D1480235

RECEIVED

MAY 2 2 2009

By _____

IN THE VALLEY OF THE KINGS

IN THE VALLEY
OF THE KINGS

HOWARD CARTER *and the* MYSTERY
of KING TUTANKHAMUN'S TOMB

DANIEL MEYERSON

BALLANTINE BOOKS · *New York*

Published in the United States by Ballantine Books, an imprint
of The Random House Publishing Group, a division of
Random House, Inc., New York.

BALLANTINE and colophon are registered trademarks of
Random House, Inc.

Library of Congress Cataloging-in-Publication Data
Meyerson, Daniel.
In the valley of the kings : Howard Carter and the mystery of
King Tutankhamun's tomb / Daniel Meyerson.
        p.   cm.
Includes bibliographical references and index.
ISBN 978-0-345-47693-7 (hardcover : alk. paper)
1. Carter, Howard, 1874–1939. 2. Egyptologists—Great Britain—Biography.
3. Tutankhamen, King of Egypt—Tomb. 4. Excavations (Archaeology)—
Egypt—Valley of the Kings. I. Title.
PJ1064.C3M49 2009
932'.01492—dc22
    [B]   2009013176

Printed in the United States of America on acid-free paper

www.ballantinebooks.com

2 4 6 8 9 7 5 3 1

FIRST EDITION

Book design by Simon M. Sullivan

For
PHILLIPE, (AL)CHEMIST EXTRAORDINAIRE
and
MUSTAFA KAMIL

I HAVE SEEN YESTERDAY. I KNOW TOMORROW.

—INSCRIPTION IN THE TOMB OF
PHARAOH TUTANKHAMUN, 1338 BC

CONTENTS

A NOTE ON THE MAP OF EGYPT

There are two sources for the Nile—one is in Uganda, the other in the Ethiopian highlands. The "two" Niles, the Blue Nile and the White Nile, join in the Sudan, at Khartoum, and begin their long journey toward the Mediterranean. When the Nile reaches Cairo, it fans out into many branches that run through a low-lying delta region to the sea. The area around Cairo and the delta is known as Lower Egypt.

Somewhat south of Cairo (120 km south, to be exact, about a subject that is not exact), we arrive at the city of Beni Suef, which is a good conventional demarcation point between Lower Egypt and Middle Egypt. Middle Egypt may be said to run to a city on the Nile called Qus, which is 20 km north of Luxor. Upper Egypt starts here and runs south, encompassing Nubia, an area that includes northern Sudan (part of Egypt in ancient times).

Ancient Egyptians thought of their country as having two parts: Upper and Lower Egypt. Their history was said to have begun with the unification of the Two Lands (one of the names for Egypt) when the king of Upper Egypt conquered the north. This duality was reflected in countless ways in Egyptian iconography, most prominently seen in the pharaoh's Double Crown. The basketlike Red Crown, symbol of the north, would be worn inside the cone-shaped White Crown of the south.

Over time, the north/south duality became part of the multifaceted dialectic that obsessed Egyptian thought: North/south, barren desert/fertile farmland, birth/death were not merely facts of life, but inspired art, ritual, and myth for this imaginative, speculative people.

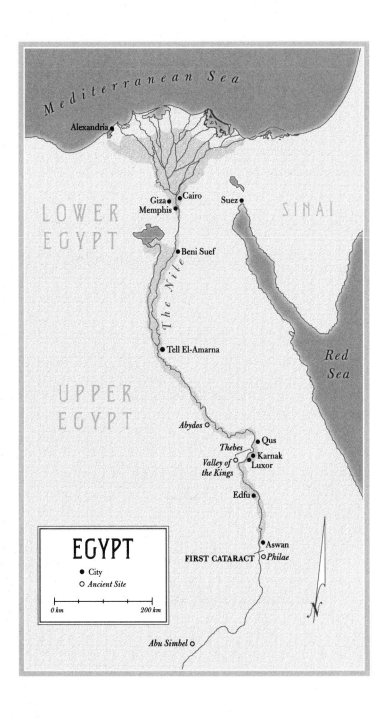

Mediterranean Sea

Alexandria

LOWER EGYPT

Giza
Cairo
Memphis
Suez

SINAI

Beni Suef

The Nile

Tell El-Amarna

UPPER EGYPT

Red Sea

Abydos

Thebes
Qus
Valley of the Kings
Karnak
Luxor

Edfu

EGYPT

● City
○ Ancient Site

0 km   200 km

Aswan
FIRST CATARACT ○ Philae

N

Abu Simbel ○

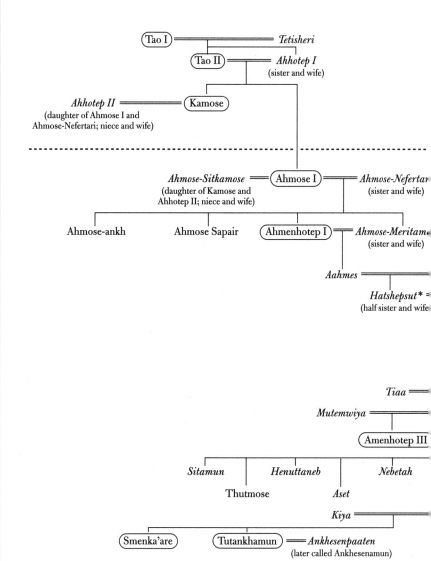

Tao I ══════════ *Tetisheri*

      Tao II ══════ *Ahhotep I*
               (sister and wife)

Ahhotep II ══════════ Kamose
(daughter of Ahmose I and
Ahmose-Nefertari; niece and wife)

- -

Ahmose-Sitkamose ═══ Ahmose I ══ *Ahmose-Nefertari*
(daughter of Kamose and   (sister and wife)
Ahhotep II; niece and wife)

Ahmose-ankh   Ahmose Sapair   Ahmenhotep I ══ *Ahmose-Meritamun*
                                           (sister and wife)

Aahmes ══════════

Hatshepsut* ═
(half sister and wife)

Tiaa ══════

Mutemwiya ══════

Amenhotep III

Sitamun   *Henuttaneb*   *Nebetah*
    Thutmose   *Aset*

Kiya ══════

Smenka'are   Tutankhamun ══ *Ankhesenpaaten*
                          (later called Ankhesenamun)

? ══════

Meritaten Tasher

TUTANKHAMUN'S FAMILY TREE

(Pharaoh) Male *Female*

═══ marriage ——— offspring

? ═══ *Senseneb*

═(Thutmose I) ═══ *Mutnofret*

═══ (Thutmose II) ═══ *Iset*

Neferure

Hatshepsut-Meryetre ═══ (Thutmose III)
ot Hatshepsut's daughter)

═══ (Amenhotep II)

═(Thutmose IV)   *Yuya* ═══ Tjuyu

═══ *Tiye*   Anen

Beketaten   (Kheperkheprure Ay) ═══ *Tey*

═(Akhenaten) ═══ *Nefertiti*   *Mutnedjmet* ═══ (Horemheb) ═══ *Amenia*

Meketaten   *Neferneferuaten*   *Neferneferure*   *Setepenre*
                Tasherit

═══ *Meritaten*   *Ankhesenamun* ═══ ?

Ankhesenpaaten
Tasherit

* Hatshepsut usurped power and became a pharaoh.

PART ONE

EXPENSES PAID AND NOTHING ELSE (BUT FATE)

Let the one who enters here beware.
His heart shall have no pleasure in life.
—NEW KINGDOM TOMB CURSE

CHAPTER 1

New Year's Day 1901
Deir el-Bahri, Southern Egypt

EVERYONE WHO WAS ANYONE WAS IN THE DESERT THAT DAY. AN excited crowd had gathered beneath the stark cliffs that rose dramatically behind the two ancient temples. One was dedicated to the soul of Queen Hatshepsut, 1550 BC, and the even older one next to it, Mentuhotep I's, had stood there in the relentless sun for four thousand years.

It was a place of great desolation and silence. Behind the temples towered the lifeless cliffs; and before them, the blinding white sand stretched endlessly to meet the empty sky. *Djeser djeseru,* the ancients called it, the holy of holies, the dwelling place of Meretsinger, the cobra goddess: She Who Loves Silence.

And it was here that the noisy crowd descended, chattering, speculating, filled with the nervous restlessness of modernity. In search of sensation, treasure, beauty—how could the goddess bear them as she watched from her barren heights?

First and foremost was the British viceroy, Lord Cromer, a man whose word was law in Egypt. He'd dropped everything, leaving Cairo in the midst of one of Egypt's endless crises. After ordering his private train, he'd traveled five hundred miles south, then taken a boat across the Nile, and then a horse-drawn calèche out toward the desert valley. The price of Egyptian cotton had plummeted on the world market, pests were ravaging the crops, and starvation stalked the countryside. But what did that matter next to the fact that a royal tomb had been discovered? After months of laborious excavation, the diggers had finally reached the door of a burial chamber with its clay seals still intact—and His Lordship wanted to be present at the opening.

As did an assortment of idle princes, pashas, and high-living riffraff from the international moneyed scene . . . along with the usual hangers-on of the very rich: practitioners of the world's oldest profession. Which in Egypt didn't refer to—to what it usually does, but meant grave robbers (or archaeologists, as they are more politely known).

To dig with any success ("to excavate," in the polite lingo), one needed knowledge. And one needed money—a great deal of it.

Thus, they often came in pairs, the archaeologists and their sugar daddies. There were famous "couples"—inseparables for all their differences of temperament and background. For example, looking back on turn-of-the-century Egyptology, can one think of the American millionaire Theodore Davis apart from the young Cambridge scholar Edward Ayrton?

Together they discovered a long list of tombs and burial shafts, Pharaoh Horemheb's, Pharaoh Siptah's, and "the golden tomb" (KV #56)* among them. As well as the mysterious Tomb Kings Valley #55—and the animal tombs (#50, #51, and #52): the mummified and bejeweled pets of Amenhotep II. The beloved crea-

---

* The tombs in the Valley of the Kings are numbered from one to sixty-two. The general rule is that tombs with lower numbers have either lain open since antiquity or were discovered earlier than those higher in the sequence. The tombs in the adjoining valleys (the Valley of the Queens, the Nobles, the West Valley, and Deir el-Bahri) are referred to by their own numbering sequences. DB #320, for example, refers to tomb number 320 from the Deir el-Bahri sequence. It is to John Gardner Wilkinson that we owe the numbering system still in use. In the 1820s and 1830s, Wilkinson lived in Gurneh, at the edge of the Valley of the Kings, where he studied those tombs that were accessible and devised his numbering system.

tures had been stripped of their jewelry by ancient robbers who had even decided to create a "joke"—perhaps the oldest in existence—leaving pharaoh's monkey and dog face-to-face. Which was how Davis and Ayrton found them some three thousand years later: locked in an eternal stand-off.

The two men, the millionaire and the scholar, made a striking picture: Davis, headstrong, determined, unwilling to be denied anything he wanted. The entrepreneur stood erect, staring down the camera in his flared riding pants and polished boots and gray side whiskers; Ayrton stood next to him, athletic, boyish, shy, a straw boater tilted at a rakish angle as he smiled absentmindedly, staring out over the desert. If it wasn't exactly a marriage made in heaven—the two had their ups and downs—still their partnership produced significant results.

Or take Howard Carter and Lord Carnarvon, another such couple. Carter, irascible to the point of being rabid when the fit was on him, intense, brooding, obsessed. With almost no formal education and a humble background, he was the quintessential outsider whose artistic ability was his one saving grace. Where would he have been without his Earl of Carnarvon, the lovable "Porchy"— bon vivant heir to a thirty-six-thousand-acre estate who came to the excavations supplied with fine china, table linen, and the best wines?

Though they tried to pass themselves off as patrons of the arts and archaeology, the truth was that these high rollers were not selfless. They paid for an excavation because they stood to gain a great deal from it, more than they would have at the racetracks and roulette tables of their usual watering holes.

The laws—or, better, the rules of the game—in Egypt allowed for an equal division of whatever was found: statues, jewelry, papyri. The fledgling Egyptian Museum at Cairo got half the take, the other half went to the wealthy diggers. It was this prospect that drew the British earls and American millionaires to the remote desert wadis with their magnificent treasures . . . and their ancient curses and gods.

There was, however, one exception in this high-stakes game, the wild card in the deck: an intact royal burial. A pharaoh's tomb or a queen's sepulcher undisturbed since the time of its sealing. In the case of such a discovery, all bets were off and the rules changed. In theory, everything went to the Egyptian Museum— though what would happen in practice no one knew, since up to that time such a discovery had never been made. What was more, it was such a remote possibility that those in the know discounted it. The tombs found so far had all been at least partially plundered in antiquity.

But this discouraged no one, since a plundered tomb could be astonishing enough. What had been worthless to the ancient thieves was often worth a fortune to their modern counterparts. The early grave robbers concentrated on gold and silver, or on jars filled with costly perfumes and unguents. They would pour the oils into animal skins to be easily carried away, leaving behind exquisite works of art. They couldn't have fenced the finely carved statues. Or the limestone and alabaster sarcophagi, the painted coffins and splendidly illustrated rolls of papyri. Such priceless leavings made the game well worthwhile (a game that in modern terms came to hundreds of thousands of British pounds, or American dollars, or French francs).

Then, too, there were the accidental finds stumbled upon in such "plundered" tombs: amulets overlooked in the folds of mummy wrappings or jewelry dropped in the haste of an ancient getaway. A "worthless" crocodile mummy, brittle to the touch, would crack open to reveal a hundred-foot papyrus roll, a masterpiece of the calligrapher's art. A mummified arm would be discovered—the arm of Queen Mernneith, broken from her body and thrust into a niche during the First Dynasty (3000 BC). Laden

with wondrously worked golden bracelets, the arm had been plastered over by some hapless thief who'd never managed to return
for his booty. His loss was his modern "brother's" gain (the severe
and Spartan W. Flinders Petrie, working over the supposedly exhausted Abydos site with a fine-tooth comb).

With so much at stake, is it any wonder that Egypt was a place
of feverish rumors and speculation? Competition was fierce:
among private collectors, among dealers in antiquities (both real
ones and forgeries), and among the great museums of the world.
The Louvre, the British Museum, and the Metropolitan Museum
of Art all had their unscrupulous representatives at work. Greedy,
squabbling children, they were anxious to obtain the finest examples of ancient art: provenance known or unknown—no questions
asked.

Of course, they were all there in the desert on that hot, bright
November day. The opening of an intact royal tomb was not an
event they were likely to miss. Nor would the "father" of this
naughty family overlook such an occasion: Gaston Maspero, the
mudir, or director, of the Service des Antiquités, a devoted scholar
whose job it was to keep his acquisitive children in check.

Portly, middle-aged, unworldly—a French academic—Maspero
had come to Egypt in 1881 to become the second director of the
newly established service. His position as mudir had forced him
quickly to learn the ins and outs of the shady antiquities markets.

His first task had been a very "unacademic one": to trace the
source of a steady stream of treasure, recognizably from royal burials, that had been showing up on the market. With the help of a
wealthy American collector (Charles Wilbour) and an agent working for both Russia and Belgium (Mustafa Aga Ayat), Maspero followed a torturous trail. It began with two leather strips, outer
mummy wrappings, and led to a notorious grave-robbing family,
the Abd er Rassuls.

Maspero had its members "interrogated" roughly. For though

he was soft-spoken and humane, when it came to saving antiquities he could be as hard as nails. He ordered a bastinado for the culprits, a beating on the soles of their feet. Ironically, it was a harsher method than the one used on the ancient grave robbers, who were merely lashed on the back to make them talk (the blows given by the hundred, one wound counting as five blows). The bastinado, though, besides causing the whole body to swell, created extreme mental anguish. It left Ahmad er Rassul, the brother who finally confessed, crippled for life (afterward, Maspero was clever enough to recruit him as a service inspector).

The disclosures led to the discovery of a remote desert tomb known as the Deir el-Bahri cache—the hiding place of thirty royal mummies, among them Amenhotep I; Thutmosis I, II, and III; Seti I; Ramesses II and III; and the royal family of the priest-pharaoh Pinedjem. During the breakdown of order in Egypt (in the Twentieth and Twenty-first dynasties), the royal mummies had been taken from their tombs by priests striving to protect their sacred god-kings. Moved from place to place, they were finally reburied here, DB tomb #320.

Here they had remained for three thousand years—and might have remained forever if not for some roaming Arabs. One idly threw a stone into a cleft in the face of the cliffs, and the hollow ringing echo alerted an er Rassul brother who was with them. Keeping his suspicions to himself, he frightened his companions with talk of demons and ghosts in the area. Then he and his brothers returned to investigate. As a result, the er Rassuls had been selling the tomb's treasures bit by bit for over a decade.

Maspero had the royal mummies taken upriver to Cairo. They made the long trip to wailing all along the way, "the women screaming and tearing their hair," as Emile Brugsch, Maspero's assistant, wrote. The peasants crowded to the riverbank, filling the air with a ritual lamentation. Their stylized wailing went back to the earliest epochs of history, when the pharaoh's death was an act of cosmic significance: It represented the death of a god, the eclipse of the sun, a time of danger and instability. Perhaps moved by some obscure instinct, the mourning villagers now reenacted the same scene that had taken place thousands of years before.

Once in Cairo, the mummies were eventually studied with the most up-to-date scientific methods of the time.* The notes scrawled on their coffins were translated and the history of their wanderings recorded. Finally put on display, their expressive features—faces from another world—were gazed upon by an admiring multitude. And thus Maspero began his directorship of the service with a resounding success.

Maspero's position plunged him into the thick of Egyptian politics. Among his many responsibilities was the granting of concessions to excavate. It was up to him to decide which ancient sites went to whom. National passions were at their height in the years before World War I, and the claims of British diggers had to be considered against French ones, not to mention American, Italian, and German rivalries. Complicating matters was the fact that the British exercised political control over Egypt, while the French had been culturally preeminent in the country since Napoleon's invasion a century before.

By nationality Maspero was French; by extraction he was Italian; and in his sympathies he was Anglophile. But the cause closest to his heart was knowledge. He sought to strengthen the service, hoping in this way to preserve the ancient sites and to stop the unrestrained looting of Egypt's treasures.

---

* Over the next decades, the study of mummies would make great progress. The first X-raying of mummies was performed by William Flinders Petrie in 1898. By 1911, Sir Armand Ruffer, a French baron and professor of medicine in Cairo, had developed a technique for preventing brittle ancient mummy tissue from crumbling under the microscope. And the autopsies Dr. Grafton Elliot Smith of the Cairo School of Medicine performed on the royal mummies were all meticulously recorded and published.

A beautifully wrought work of art had a monetary value on the antiquities market. But when exact information as to where it had been found could be obtained—when it could be put into a historical context—its scientific value increased tenfold.

Both realist and idealist, Maspero knew that money was the key. Money not only to excavate, but also to preserve what had already been uncovered. To guard the temples and tombs, to restore them, to record the inscriptions covering their walls. Since scant public funds were available, private contributions were a necessity—and such contributions often had to come from the very people he had to be most wary of.

In pursuit of his goals, the new director cultivated a wide range of friendships, anyone and everyone who could be of help. There were the poor itinerant scholars: men and women wandering among the ruins, notebooks in hand, their families moving from pension to pension (figures such as James Breasted, whose translations of ancient inscriptions in Egypt and Nubia ran into many volumes and remain a standard work; his son Charles recalls meager meals in backstreet Egyptian restaurants, his parents dividing the food among the three of them with a careful hand).

And there were the wealthy itinerant aristocrats—an international crowd wintering in Egypt. They sailed the Nile on luxurious dahabiyyas or were pampered in fantastically opulent hotels such as Shepherd's in Cairo or Luxor's Winter Palace. Maspero was always a welcome presence among them: earnest but never gauche; witty and sociable.

He enlisted the help of pious churchmen, reverends eager to prove the historical truth of the Bible; and he employed impious thieves of every stripe and rank, high and low. An embassy clerk might pass on a tip as to what was being smuggled out in the diplomatic pouch: a rare scarab, a pharaonic diadem, or a bust such as the famous one of Nefertiti that was brought to Berlin in this way.

It is a wonder that Maspero, understaffed and overworked, had the energy not only to fulfill his duties as mudir so brilliantly, but at the same time to pursue his scholarship. But somehow he did—keeping one eye on the fashionable guest list of Shepherd's Hotel and the other on a papyrus scroll. His knowledge of the monuments was encyclopedic, his writings were prolific, and his work on the pyramid texts was groundbreaking. He was first among the Egyptologists of his generation, at the same time taking under his wing many young hopefuls of the next.

Among those Maspero encouraged was Howard Carter, though the young man fit into none of the usual categories. He had no education, no money, no family background, and no training in Egyptology. He could speak neither Arabic nor French, and his manners were awkward and abrupt. He was taciturn, brooding, and bad-tempered. He didn't even have the robust constitution required for turn-of-the-century archaeology, when diggers lived for months on tinned food, sleeping in tents or ancient tombs cut into the cliffs. He had nothing but his stubbornness, an iron determination to make good.

His roots were rural and lower class. His grandfather had been gamekeeper on a Norfolk country estate, where his family had lived for generations. Carter's father, Samuel, had been the one to break away, developing his natural gifts to become a painter specializing in animal portraits.

Carter would write of him in later years (in an autobiographical sketch or journal he never published): "He was one of the most powerful draughtsmen I ever knew. His knowledge of comparative anatomy and memory for form was [*sic*] matchless. He could depict from memory, accurately, any animal in any action, foreshortened or otherwise, with the greatest ease."

To this he added a word of professional criticism: "However, if a son may criticize his father, this faculty was in many ways his misfortune. For by it he was not so obliged to seek nature as much as an artist should, hence his art became somewhat styled as well as period marked."

Whatever his merits or faults as a painter, the elder Carter had enough admirers to make a career for himself. He worked in the great country houses, painting the beloved horses of the aristocrats; and he worked as an artist for the *Illustrated Times* as well, supplying sketches and drawings for the London newspaper. This eventually necessitated his moving to London with his large family and his animal models (penned up behind the house).

Howard Carter, however, was raised by a maiden aunt in Norfolk. He was a sickly child, and it was thought that the country air would strengthen him. What's more, such an arrangement eased the financial strain, Carter being the youngest of eleven brothers and sisters.

His formal education was cut short after a few years in a simple rural school in Norfolk where he learned the basics. He wrote later that this was due to ill health, but the real reason was probably financial. It was necessary for Carter to begin to make a living as soon as possible. "I have next to nothing to say about my education . . . nature thrusts some of us into the world miserably incomplete," he remarked with some bitterness in his journal. Throughout his life, he felt his lack of education. It was one of the sources of his resentment—and of his determination to succeed.

Fortunately, Carter showed early signs of having inherited a gift for sketching and painting. When his father worked in the great country houses, the young Carter began to go with him, serving a kind of informal apprenticeship. Soon, he was able to obtain small commissions of his own: "For a living, I began by drawing in water colours and coloured chalks portraits of pet parrots, cats and snappy, smelly lap dogs."

But as he sat drawing his lapdogs and parrots, fate hovered over the boy. William Tyssen-Amherst, one of his father's patrons, was an aficionado, an Egyptomaniac, an addict—call it what you will— a passionate collector. He was mad for Egypt, as was his whole family, his wife and five daughters (Mary Tyssen-Amherst, later Lady Cecil, would excavate in Aswan, uncovering a significant cache of late Ptolemaic papyri, among other finds).

Didlington Hall, the Tyssen-Amherst estate, housed some of the most important Egyptian antiquities in private hands. As you approached the manor on its south side, you passed through a formal garden. Here, seven massive black statues loomed amid the flower beds and gravel paths. Fashioned in the fourteenth century BC for Amenhotep III—Tutankhamun's grandfather—they were signifiers of a different reality: images of Sekhmet, a goddess who tore men to pieces at the request of the sun, her lithe, bare-breasted body joined to a lion's head.

They were a hint of what was in the great hall: the vividly painted coffins and shawabti (magical figures, "answerers" who would come to life at the utterance of a spell); the wonderful statues from almost every period in Egypt's history. Some, like the block statue of Senwosret-Senebefny, Overseer of the Reckoning of the Cattle, were covered with biographical inscriptions. The Overseer is a powerful figure, whose strong limbs, or a suggestion of them, can be seen just under his robe, a marvel of the sculptor's art (Twelfth Dynasty, ca. 1800 BC).

For two years, from age fifteen to seventeen, Carter was a frequent visitor at the estate, becoming a favorite of the family. From a sketch his father made of him at the time, we can see the boy: An enormous white collar falls over his buttoned-up wool jacket, his longish wavy hair is parted on one side, his eyes are large and dreamy. When not occupied with his work, Carter drew the gods and goddesses, the mummies and coffins; his sketchbooks from this period are filled with them. He was developing a feeling for

Egyptian art—he was "hooked": "It was the Amherst Egyptian Collection at Didlington Hall," he later wrote, "that aroused my longing for that country. It gave me an earnest desire to see Egypt."

Just as important to him as the works of art were Tyssen-Amherst's papyri. How could they fail to capture the boy's imagination? Translated by the foremost scholars of the day, they included poems and songs and sacred texts beautifully illustrated— the Book of the Dead, and the Book of Gates, and the Book of What Is in the Underworld—and the harsh drama of an ancient grave-robbing trial known simply as the Amherst papyrus. Written in hieratic—a flowing script, a kind of shorthand hieroglyphs— the transcript records a trial that took place during the reign of Ramesses IX (Twentieth Dynasty, 1120–1108 BC).

Charged with plundering the tomb of Pharaoh Sobekemsaf, an ancient tomb even then (Thirteenth Dynasty), the stonemason Amunpanefer at first denied everything. But when he was beaten again and again with a double rod ("Give him the stick! The stick!"), he finally confessed. We can almost hear him cry out: "We found the noble mummy of this king with a sword. There were many amulets and jewels of gold upon his neck . . . and his mask of gold was upon him. The noble mummy of this god was completely covered with gold and his coffins were adorned with gold and silver, inside and out, and with every costly stone. We stripped off the gold that we found on the august mummy of this god, and its amulets and ornaments that were at its throat, and we set fire to the coverings. . . ."

This trial was one of many, since the lure of the treasure was irresistible, as other ancient transcripts reveal: "We went up in a single body. The foreigner Nesamun showed us the tomb of Ramesses VI, the Great God. We said to him, Where is the tomb maker who was with you? And he said to us: He was killed. . . .

"I spent four days breaking into the tomb, there being five of us.

We opened the tomb and we entered it. We found a basket lying on sixty chests. . . . We opened them and found . . .

"My father ferried the thieves over to the island of Amunemopet and they said to him, This inner coffin is ours. It belonged to some great person. We were hungry and we went and brought it away, but you be silent and we will give you a loincloth. So they said to him. And they gave him a loincloth. But my mother said to him, You are a silly old man. What you have done is stealing."

Later, such documents would be important clues when Carter began to piece together his deductions about the royal necropolis (city of the dead). But for now, he was just becoming familiar with the long-dead figures: the Ramesses and Setis and Amenhoteps who would, for the next forty-five years, be his all-consuming passion. There would be no great love in his life, not even a passing romance. No wife, no mistress, no children. The tombs he uncovered were to be the main events of his life, a long list of them leading toward the great prize: a royal tomb, almost untouched—as his sixth sense told him it would be—and filled with breathtakingly beautiful objects.

To the young Carter, though, Egypt seemed as far away as the moon. The Tyssen-Amherst collection had fired his imagination, but there matters ended. The scholars and professors who visited at Didlington Hall were in a different category from his. They were equals who had come to talk learnedly about the antiquities. In class-conscious England, Carter was a step above the servants; his job was to sketch Tyssen-Amherst's favorite animals.

Ironically enough, his lack of education—his being "miserably incomplete," as he put it—would give him his first break. His services could be obtained cheaply, which was just what the recently founded Egyptian Exploration Fund needed. They could not afford to hire another expensive gentleman-scholar.

Engaged in an epic project, the fund had been recording the

countless ancient inscriptions and friezes endangered by vandals, flooding, fading, and the like. Photography could capture just so much, given the limited techniques of the time. To copy the paintings in the long, winding passages of the dark tombs, to record the rows of hieroglyphics on temple walls, to faithfully reproduce colors and details, artists were needed. The fund had a team working in the rock tombs of Beni Hasan (Middle Egypt). But the work had lagged, and an extra hand was needed.

One of the fund's directors wrote to John Newberry (whose brother, Percy Newberry, was a Cambridge-trained Egyptologist working for the fund at Beni Hasan): "If you come across a colourist (eye for colour must be chief qualification added to drawing) who would like a trip to Egypt for expenses paid and nothing else, I should be much obliged if you would ask him to call. . . . It seems to me that as cost is a great consideration it matters not whether the artist is a gentleman or not. Your brother [Percy Newberry] can fraternize with George Willoughby Fraser [another member of the Beni Hasan team and a 'gentleman']. . . . A gentleman unless of an economical turn of mind would run into extra expenses very likely, while if a non-gentleman were sent out Percy Newberry could take him under his wing and manage all his feeding etc. as his employer. In this way 2 or 3 shillings might be saved daily."

As it happened, Percy Newberry was on leave in England at the time, and his brother forwarded the letter to him. Since Newberry frequently visited at Didlington Hall, he immediately thought of Carter. He had seen his work and thought it was "good enough"; moreover, he liked the boy.

Tyssen-Amherst seconded the idea, so the matter was settled. Carter was to spend the summer training at the British Museum, where he would carefully study the precise and beautiful drawings done in the beginning of the century by Robert Hay, one of the first Europeans to have explored the ruins of Egypt.

Whatever training he received was picked up hastily, during these few summer months. Francis Llewellyn Griffith, superintendent of the Archaeological Survey, tried to prepare him as best he could, along with C. H. Read. "These venerable people," Carter recalled later, "and this august building with its associations and its resonant rooms, deeply impressed me and produced an awe that caused me to be in a mortal funk lest my boots squeaked." His boots well oiled—presumably—here he learned more about the lines of Egyptian art and the hieroglyphic writing he would be copying.

Then, at the end of those three months in 1892—Carter was seventeen years old—his new life began.

CHAPTER 2

ALMOST A DECADE LATER, THE CARTER OF 1901 STOOD BE-fore the tomb he had discovered. Though still not considered a gentleman by the standards of his countrymen, he could give a good imitation of one. At least he was considered passable company: His colleagues fraternized with him, albeit with a patronizing attitude.

He was formally attired, though he was in the middle of the desert, as were the others who had gathered for the opening of "his" tomb—that is, the intact royal tomb he had discovered.

With nothing more than a hunch to go on, he'd struggled for two years to organize an expedition. Every step of the way had been fraught with difficulties, from finding a backer to pay for the dig, to getting the Department of Antiquities' permission to work the site,* to the excavation itself, which proved unbelievably complicated.

Hundreds of feet underground, at the end of a long, descending

---

* With the establishment of the Egyptian Antiquities Service in 1858, permission to excavate had to be sought from the Department of Antiquities. Such permission, called a concession, marked out the area to be explored and stipulated the terms under which the excavator could dig and how he or she had to proceed in the event of a tomb being discovered. In 1902, the American banker Theodore Davis took on the concession to dig in the main Valley of the Kings, a concession he would not relinquish until shortly before World War I.

passage, he had finally uncovered a vast, almost empty chamber after months of digging. Leading down from this chamber was a sunken shaft that was so deep, it took two seasons to clear it. But clear it he finally did, coming upon a door stamped with the seal of the royal necropolis: a recumbent jackal, Anubis, god of mummification, over nine bound prisoners.

This sealed doorway, and the unbreached underground stone wall on either side of it (twelve feet thick), caused him to summon the consul, the Egyptian prime minister, the head of the Antiquities Service, and the experts: Carter had made an unprecedented find.

If he was nervous, he did not show it: On public occasions he was known for his self-possession. From the shy boy in the British Museum, trembling lest his boots squeak, he had developed what Emma Andrews (traveling companion of the millionaire Theodore Davis) called "a dominant personality." For almost a decade now, the Egyptian desert had been his home; he knew its terrain well, had explored its most remote valleys and lived in its tombs (sometimes sleeping in the ancient sepulchers when no other shelter was available, then a common practice).

From Carter's notebooks it can be seen that nothing escaped his notice: the quality of the rock; the patterns of flash floods in the desert (over the centuries, sudden violent torrents moved great boulders and masses of debris, covering tomb entrances and burying temples and ruins); the ancient graffiti scrawled on the cliffs—secret "markers" left by priests, doodlings and caricatures scratched by necropolis workers and guards, comments by Greek pilgrims and Roman passersby; and the wildlife to be found in the desert, which especially appealed to him: "some scaly, a few furred like the fox and the desert hare, but mostly feathered. Several kinds of vultures, one or two falcons, a long-legged buzzard, ravens, blue rock pigeons, sand partridge and other smaller desert birds which delight in eking out a precarious existence in desolate solitude. On high eagles soared in the still air. And along the riverbank in the scant patches of palm were turtle doves."

It was the one pleasure he allowed himself when he could: riding out on horseback to explore and to sketch. On one of these outings two years earlier (1898), his horse stumbled and fell. Unhurt, he got up to investigate. As he described it in the report he filed for the service (*Annales du Service des Antiquités de l'Égypte* II [1901]): "The ground gave way under the horse's legs bringing both of us down. Afterwards, on looking into the small hole there formed, I saw traces of stone work, from which I concluded that there must be something and most probably a tomb. I commenced excavating on the 20th January, 1900, in order to find out what really was there, and in a short time, I was able to trace the three sides of the stone work, the fourth side, to the east, being open. From this state of the east end, I concluded that, if it was a tomb, the entrance would be below the western end, so I at once set the men to work there. . . ."

In his report, he quickly moved from the fateful fall in the desert to the excavation. But two years intervened before he was able to raise the funds for the excavation. His immediate superior at the time, the scholar Édouard Naville, was skeptical. As Carter remembered in his journal: "All that I received for my pains was a somewhat splenetic remark, that had a taint of ridicule."

Carter shrugged off Professor Naville's ridicule, however, and tried to raise money to dig. He won over Maspero, who found some money for him and then convinced an unidentified sponsor to step forward with the rest.

The excavation turned out to be more difficult than anyone had imagined. More and more workers had to be engaged, hundreds of men. The subterranean corridors were hundreds of feet long and cut deep beneath the ground. There were stone-blocking walls twelve feet in thickness and sharp salt stalagmites that had formed out of the rock, obstructing the passage. Finally, Carter reached not the burial chamber but a huge, vaulted room some 56 feet belowground. From this room a vertical shaft led down more than 320 feet to yet another corridor below. The area to be excavated was vast, and the amount of earth and stone to be removed was enormous.

"After working down some 17 metres [56 feet]," as Carter told it, "I found the door which had its original mud brick sealings intact. I made a small hole at the top of the door and entered, finding myself in a long arched passage having a downward incline of about 1 in 5. Inside the door, a head of a calf and portions of a calf's leg were lying on the floor [the remains of four-thousand-year-old sacrificial offerings]. I descended the passage, which was quite clear and 150 metres [492 feet] long, ending in a large lofty chamber, the roof again arched. . . .

"In the left hand corner, lying on its side was a seated statue . . . completely wrapped in linen of a very fine quality: beside it lay a long wooden coffin which was inscribed but bore no name. . . . The style of the work shewed that the tomb was of the early Theban empire [2010 BC]. Along the end wall and in the centre of the chamber, pots with mud sealings, a dish and many small saucers, all of rough red pottery, together with the skeletons of two ducks? and two forelegs of a calf which still had on them the dried up flesh, were lying on the floor. Having tested the ground with a piercing rod, I found that there was a shaft leading down from the chamber.

"On the 16th of March, 1900, I started the men to open the shaft; but on the 20th of April, the shaft proved to be so deep, the rock so bad and becoming so dangerous that I was obliged to stop the work until the next season. . . ."

It was impossible to work in the valley during the summer; the temperatures rose to 120 degrees or more. He was forced to wait for the fall to see what the burial chamber at the bottom of the shaft held. Apart from the intact seals on the outer door, the statue he had found was a good augur. It was massive, powerful, the figure of a king seated on his throne and dressed in the short white cloak worn during the heb-sed, or thirty-year jubilee festival, when the god-king renewed his powers.

"I am hard at work," he wrote to Lady Tyssen-Amherst, "trying to get to the bottom of the tomb I found at Deir el-Bahri last year. I trust to manage it soon though under difficulties—the men have now got down 97 metres [320 feet] vertical drop and still no end, but cannot help but think the end will come soon; then there are chances of a good find, it being untouched. . . ."

"Consider the circumstances," he noted in his journal, "a young excavator, all alone except for his workmen, on the threshold of a magnificent discovery."

To really understand what this moment meant—it was everything for him, the reason for his existence—it is necessary to keep in mind what had gone into its making: the years of preparation, the work carried out in difficult conditions, the sweltering heat in the south, the swarms of insects in the Delta, the lack of creature comforts, the living in tents and tombs when no other shelter was available.

By day, the labor was backbreaking, painstaking, grueling: There was the endless digging and sifting, often yielding nothing but a handful of dust; the crawling and clambering through suffocating underground passages filled with thousands of bats, centuries of their waste creating a poisonous atmosphere; the unstable shale under the solid limestone threatening to collapse. Death or crippling accidents were an ever-present danger.

The work continued by night, though it was of a different sort. After doctoring the men, settling disputes, photographing finds, carrying out whatever immediate preservation was required for the most fragile finds, and so forth—after the countless tasks for which the excavator was responsible, there was the bookkeeping. Long hours in his tent or tomb going over the figures and writing out records of expenses: workmen's wages, daily expenses—outlays for equipment damaged, food for the pack animals, rewards to the workers for anything found (to prevent pilferage), and the like. On a large dig with hundreds of workmen, especially when payments were made not by time but by the area cleared or the levels dug, the accounting could become bewilderingly complicated.

This was followed by more bookkeeping, equally tedious, though of an archaeological sort: the careful, almost obsessive noting of every detail of the day's work. Everything must be recorded, nothing was too trivial. For what at the moment may seem insignificant could take on an unimagined importance later on. A decorative pattern painstakingly preserved—the rishi, or feather design, on a coffin's decaying wood; or the position of thousands of beads on a piece of linen that had fallen apart at the touch. The shape of pottery shards tossed into a burial shaft. An ancient workman's mark scratched on the wall of a tomb; or the kinds of animal bones left from a funeral meal.

This done, there was study. Carter learned his history and his Arabic on the job and whatever hieroglyphs were essential (he would never be proficient in the ancient language, his focus being on the terrain, the wadis and cliffs and valleys). Cramming like a schoolboy for a test, he put in long hours to understand the southern valleys that had increasingly become the center of his interest, the Valley of the Kings and the areas immediately bordering it: the Valley of the Queens, the Valley of the Nobles, Dra Abu el-Naga, the Assasif, the Birabi, the Deir el-Bahri.

Here in antiquity a fateful innovation took place. The massive stone pyramids of the Old Kingdom (2680–2180 BC) had proven no barrier to the grave robbers' skill and were finally abandoned. In their stead, hidden underground tombs were created. By the time of the New Kingdom (1550 BC), these tombs were the rule. As Thutmosis I's architect Ineni boasts on his funeral stela, "I planned the tomb of the pharaoh secretly, no one hearing, no one seeing." For over five hundred years, the Valley was the scene of such secret royal burials. The hope was that pharaoh, suitably provided for in death, would join his fellow gods in eternity and see to the well-being of the land.

Huge chambers were hewn underground or in the desert cliffs and filled with treasure: jewels and gold and silver in amounts almost beyond belief. Egypt's vast wealth was poured into these tombs—and Egypt was a country where "gold is as plentiful as dust," as the king of Mitanni (an ally) wrote to Pharaoh Amenhotep III in a "begging" letter preserved in the ancient archives.

It was not only the monetary value of this treasure that kept Carter at work into the small hours of the night, but also its beauty. For the artistic impulse was very strong in Carter—he was alive to the marvels of ancient Egyptian art. From the very beginning of his career, his notebooks are filled with comments about form and color and design.

This sensitivity extended to his natural surroundings as well, the desert landscape that he lovingly sketched and painted. In fact, it was this highly developed aesthetic sense that helped him to bear the solitude of the excavator's life. For though Carter glossed over it quickly in his memoir—"a young excavator, all alone except for his workmen, on the threshold of a magnificent discovery"—this unrelieved solitude had led more than one excavator to quit because they found it unbearable.

It was as much a spiritual solitude as a geographic one. An unbridgeable distance existed between the foreign archaeologists and the Egyptian fellahin, or native peasants, who worked for them. It was felt even by an excavator as close to his workers as Flinders Petrie, Carter's most important mentor in Egypt. There are passages in Petrie's memoirs where he admired the peasants' exuberance and simplicity. He sympathized with their difficulties; he harshly criticized those archaeologists who dealt with them as if they were machines to sift and haul and dig; and he shocked his colleagues by having, in his words, "gone some way toward the fel-lahin" (that is, dispensed with formalities that most Europeans considered essential).

In his description of Egypt at that time, Petrie described the alienation, even the menace, felt by excavators living in remote vil-lages and at desert sites. "There is the lack of intercommunication, the suspicion of strangers; the absence of roads; and the mental state of the people. . . . The man who can read and write is the rare exception in the country. . . . There is gross superstition, innumer-able local saints. . . .

"We [Europeans] cannot see the world as a fellah sees it; and I believe this the more readily because after living years among the fellahin . . . I yet feel the gulf between their nature and my own as impassable as ever. . . .

"In the villages, derwish parties are formed from a few men and boys, perhaps a dozen or twenty: they are almost always held in moonlight. . . . The people stand in a circle and begin repeating Al-láh with a very strong accent on the latter syllable; bowing down the head and body at the former, and raising it at the latter. This is done all in unison, and slowly at first; gradually the rate quickens, the accent is stronger, and becomes more of an explosive howl, sounding afar off. . . . The excitement is wilder, hideously wild, until a horrid creeping comes over you as you listen and you feel that in such a state there is no answering for what may be done. In-cipient madness of the intoxication of excitement seems poured out upon them all. . . .

"The children unintentionally reveal what is the tone and talk of the households in private; they constantly greet the European with wails of Ya Nusrani!, O Nazarene! The full force of which title is felt when your donkey boy urges on his beast by calling it, 'Son of a dog! Son of a pig! Son of a Nazarene!' Any abuse will do to howl at the infidel, and I have been for months shouted at across every field. . . . That a massacre of the Coptic [Egyptian] Christians was fully anticipated by them when Arabi drove out the foreigners [a failed revolt of 1882] should not be lightly forgotten.

"This fanaticism is linked with an unreasoning ferocity of punishment. I have seen a coachman suddenly seize on a street boy and for some word or gesture lash him on the bare legs with the whip again and again with all his might. . . ."

The suppressed violence of desperate poverty and thwarted national hopes could be felt on every side. The archaeologist Gertrude Caton-Thompson, a friend and admirer of Petrie's, recalled a typical outbreak near an excavation (whose finds were eventually published as *Tombs of the Courtiers and Oxyrhynkhos*): "The season's work coincided with a serious insurrection which caused anxiety in the camp, where the loyalty of our seventy to eighty workmen was uncertain. We could hear the rattle of the machine guns, 25 miles away, mounted on the roof of the American Mission Hospital in Assyiut defending itself (successfully) against a mob who had murdered three young British officers in a train and adorned the engine with their limbs. The mutiny was quelled, but not before Petrie had stocked the well-hidden hermitage [Christian, fifth century AD] with food and water, as a possible refuge."

This, then, was the atmosphere in which Carter had been living and working for a decade. Egypt was finally awakening politically. For more than two thousand years it had been, in the words of the Hebrew prophet, "a lowly kingdom" and "a broken reed"—a land dominated by foreigners. Its last native ruler, Nectanebo II, had fled to Nubia in 343 BC, where he spent his remaining years practicing magic and leaving Egypt to the conquerors who followed: Persians, Greeks, Romans, Byzantines, Ummayads, Ayyubids, Fatimids, Mamluks, Ottomans, and finally, at the end of the nineteenth century, the hated British.

One humiliation had followed another as Egypt descended into chaos and poverty. But now young Egyptians were deter-

mined to claim their birthright, and the situation was tense and explosive. Anything could trigger a furor.

In the search for a national identity, Egypt's pharaonic treasures
became a central symbol. The time was over when Empress Eu-
génie of France could deck herself out in the jewels of an ancient
Egyptian queen, or the American millionaire Theodore Davis
could use the skull of a Ramesside prince as a paperweight. When
the great nationalist leader Sa'ad Zaghlul died, the royal mummies
lay in state with him in the huge mausoleum honoring his memory.
How delicate was the position of the foreign archaeologists and
their backers, the brash, treasure-seeking capitalists counting on a
"fair division" of the fabulous spoils.

Thus, Carter's great discovery would become intertwined with
national politics: In death, the boy-king Tutankhamun would find
himself in the middle of a national upheaval, just as he had in life,
when his name was changed from Tutankhaten and he was
brought from his heretic father's court to Wast (Thebes, modern-
day Luxor) to symbolize the national revival.

If, as Carter wrote in his journal, he was "standing on the edge
of a magnificent discovery," he was also standing at the edge of a
precipice. The royal tomb belonged to Egyptians and to Egyptians
alone, it would be claimed: Despite all their backbreaking labor
and toil, the foreigners had no rights at all.

Such thoughts, though, were far from Carter on that glorious
day in 1901. Poised for victory, he stood next to the royal tomb he
had discovered. A silence fell over the crowd as he and his foreman
descended into the tomb.

The two climbed down unaided into the rocky passage, but a
kind of basket-cradle had been arranged for the descent of the consul and the other distinguished visitors. First, though, the burial
chamber's blocking had to be removed, and Carter had to enter
and survey the find.

"I had everything prepared," he later remembered. "The long

wished for moment had arrived. We were ready to penetrate the mystery behind the masonry. The foreman and I descended, and with his aid I removed the heavy limestone slabs, block by block. The door was at last open. It led directly into a small room which was partially filled with rock chips, just as the Egyptian masons had left it, but it was otherwise empty save for some pottery water jars and some pieces of wood. At first glance I felt that there must be another doorway leading to another chamber. But a cursory examination proved that there was nothing of the sort. I was filled with dismay."

As everyone waited above, he frantically searched the passage, looking for some indication of a hidden staircase or tunnel or shaft leading—he hardly knew where, since by all indications and signs, this should be the burial chamber. It had been carefully sealed, hidden hundreds of feet underground, protected with a twelve-foot-thick wall—but it was empty. His searching uncovered only a tiny miniature coffin secreted in a wall. Its inscription indicated the king for whom the tomb was dug: Mentuhotep I, one of the first kings of the Eleventh Dynasty, a pharaoh who reigned at the beginning of the Middle Kingdom (ca. 2010 BC).

Perhaps the tomb had been dug in antiquity to throw would-be robbers off the scent. Perhaps the statue wrapped in linen represented some arcane ritual burial, a magical rite to ward off death. Perhaps building the huge mortuary temple at the foot of the cliffs (erected by this same king) caused him to change his plans and dig his tomb elsewhere in the cliffs. Or perhaps the tomb was abandoned for some other reason lost to history.

Whatever the reason, Carter now had to climb into the brilliant sunlight to publicly acknowledge his defeat. Among the onlookers were those only too ready to laugh at the presumption of this outsider, for jealousy among excavators and scholars was as intense as among opera divas—or thieves.

Covered with dust, he began to make his apologies, but quickly the compassionate and fatherly Maspero intervened. As Carter was to say of the moment: "I cannot now remember, all the kind and eloquent words that came from Maspero, but his kindness during this awful moment made one realize that he was really a worthy and true friend."

Maspero's private feelings matched his public stance. He wrote in a private letter: "Carter had announced his discovery too soon to Lord Cromer. Lord Cromer came to be present at his success and he is now very saddened at not having been able to show him anything of what he foretold. I console him as best I can, for he truly is a good fellow and he does his duty very well."

Though Carter would later remember Maspero's kindness with gratitude, at the moment he was shattered. Nothing could console him. He remained at the tomb until late at night, going over and over the underground rooms in his bewilderment.

The echo of chatter and speculation faded as the intruders went their way. They left the place to the heartbroken excavator on the threshold of his magnificent discovery—and to its tutelary goddess, Meretsinger, She Who Loves Silence.

Carter was inconsolable—but the irony was that he would also be inconsolable later, when he was finally granted his heart's desire. For twenty years after this fiasco—two full decades later, in 1922—he would find his tomb. But then it would not come to him by beginner's luck, the accident of a fallen horse, or by any other gambler's sleight of hand. It would come through grueling work and suffering and faith: faith in the powers that he knew had been granted him, though the world looked at him askance.

He would be the first to uncover a tomb that had been sealed for thousands of years. He would stand in the presence of a pharaoh lying in a solid gold coffin under a gold mask of incomparable beauty: Tutankhamun Nebkheperure—Lord of the Manifestation of the Sun, the Strong Bull, Victorious, Eternal.

Here, in the small, dark rooms of this tomb, he would labor for ten long years, carefully bringing out thousands of precious objects, among them some of the most moving works of ancient Egyptian art. After which he would spend the rest of his life famous, wealthy—and embittered.

He would never excavate again. A solitary figure, idle, angry, withdrawn, he would live out his last days on the terrace of Luxor's Winter Palace. With a touch of madness? Or perhaps with truth? He would tell anyone who would listen that he knew where the much-sought-for tomb of Alexander the Great could be found. But, he would add with spite, he would take that secret with him to the grave: The world did not deserve to know it.

Between the young boy sketching his smelly lapdogs and the raging old man was a lifetime spent in grueling, unsparing work. Yes, he would discover his tomb. But the gods would give him glory, not peace. He would fulfill the words of the New Kingdom tomb curse: "Let the one who enters here beware. His heart shall have no pleasure in life."

PART TWO

NAKED UNDER AN UMBRELLA

Archaeology is not a profession but a vendetta!

—WILLIAM FLINDERS PETRIE, 1853–1942,
the father of modern archaeology, as he was later known
(also later: Sir William). Author of more than ninety books and
monographs. His methods revolutionized the way
excavations are conducted.

CHAPTER 3

1892
Cairo: The Hotel Royale, where Carter, just off the
boat from England, is introduced to Petrie

THE FIRST TIME THE YOUNG CARTER MET HIM (IN A CAIRO hotel), Petrie was dressed in his "city" clothes: a worn but still passable suit. It was buttoned up, showing just a bit of the cravat, which was knotted anyhow beneath the high white collar in fashion then. He was unforgettable with his large, generous features; his full beard and shock of black hair brushed back over a high, swarthy brow; his enormous dark eyes set wide apart; his thick lips compressed in thought. His expression was very alert— his features were stamped with intellectual passion as surely as greed or lust can be read on other men's faces.

In all the photographs from this decade, Petrie seems always to be wearing this same suit! Somehow there is an incongruity about these respectable clothes of his, as if someone had dressed up an Old Testament prophet in a suit, cravat, and high collar. It is as if at any moment his large, athletic body will burst open the worn-out cloth, revealing his larger-than-life presence.

It is more fitting for him to be naked, like some heroic figure sculpted by Michelangelo. When working inside one or another of the pyramids, at Giza or Hawara or Lisht, he would sometimes have to wade through half-flooded chambers (the water level having risen over the centuries). Or to crawl through lower passages where the heat was unbearable. At such times—for example, when measuring Khufu's great pyramid at Giza, he would "emerge just before dawn, red eyed, oxygen deprived, smelling of bat dung"— and in his birthday suit.

Which was how Carter saw him the second time the two met: As desert winds covered Petrie with a fine layer of sand, the father of modern archaeology stood in an irrigation canal, naked under an umbrella. He had just finished soaking the salt off some ancient pots, and now he was submerged up to his shoulders in the river, trying to cool off.

In this pose, he looked "rather like a water buffalo," as Amelia Edwards, another witness of the nude Petrie, affectionately recalled. As director of the Egyptian Exploration Society, Ms. Edwards had much to do with Petrie; she fell in love with the bearded buffalo-scholar—though it was "as hopeless as loving a young obelisk," she sighed in a letter to a friend.

He was as single-minded and chaste as a monk. At least for the first half of his life, he was alone with his scarabs and pots and pyramids. Until he finally met his match in the brilliant and beautiful young Hilda Urlin, the only women he held in his arms were ones he dug up from tombs and burial pits.

He was indifferent to everything except archaeology. Sleep was a waste of time. Clothing—another unfortunate necessity—must be worn until ragged. As for food: The young hopefuls who worked with him might learn much (Carter, Mace, Weigall, Quibel, Wainwright, Engelbach, and Brunton among them—the list is long). But they would suffer. They would sleep on straw pallets or wooden packing cases, and they would starve.

"I have known him to knock a hole in a tin of sardines and drink the oil before opening it. . . . I can't go on with Petrie I have got so weak and horrid from this beastly food," Arthur Weigall wrote to his wife, a complaint echoed by a chorus of hungry young archaeologists.

"Petrie was a man of forty-one with . . . the agility of a boy,"

Charles Breasted remembered. "His clothes confirmed his universal reputation for being not only careless but slovenly and dirty. He was thoroughly unkempt, clad in ragged dirty shirt and trousers, and worn-out sandals. . . . He served a table so excruciatingly bad that only persons of iron constitution could survive it; even they had been known on occasion stealthily to leave his camp in order to assuage their hunger by sharing the comparatively luxurious beans and unleavened bread of the local fellahin [peasants]. . . . The fact remains that he not only miraculously survived the consistent practice of what he preached, but established in the end a record of maximum results for minimum expenditure which is not likely to be surpassed. . . ."

There were no tinned sardines, however, at the Hotel Royale, where Petrie was staying when he first met Carter. Though it was in a good quarter of Cairo, Ezbekia, it was not the exclusive, fashionable Shepherd's Hotel. However, it had the same chef as Shepherd's, as the man had saved up and gone into business for himself. Thus, Petrie's visitors were treated to the last word in culinary refinements when they attended his nightly archaeological salon.

The many distinguished scholars, the epigraphists and geologists, the linguists and historians and excavators, not to mention Petrie's half-starved students—everyone—as the talk turned on mummy-bandaging techniques and nummulitic limestone, could gorge himself to his heart's content under Petrie's disapproving, fanatic eye.

Carter remembered those gatherings in his journal. He was awed by the company and afraid of Petrie, "a man," he noted, "who did not suffer fools." It was a phrase Amelia Edwards also used about him, adding fondly that that was because "he was born more alive than most men."

Be that as it may, at these meetings Carter was silent while Petrie talked. Petrie was in his forties, while Carter was still in his teens, and the older man theorized, pronounced, and advised about everything. Everything! From the subtleties of scarab styles to excavation guards who snore to the name of the pharaoh of the Exodus. How to deal with ancient, fragile textiles, with carbonized papyri, and with fleas.

Covering many subjects with lightning speed, Petrie held forth like an oracle in a cryptic, staccato style, backing into tables and overturning chairs when he became excited. Even the sound of his voice was oracular: It had a high and eerie quality, the way the Sibyls were said to have sounded in their trances. But though Petrie was, like them, a being possessed, there is a simpler explanation for his quavering, reedy tones—an act of violence he met with at the beginning of his career.

"Exploring on foot and alone in the Sinai desert," his colleague Gertrude Caton-Thompson related, "he was approached by three Bedouin in that empty land. He scented danger, and quickly threw his wallet by a backhand movement into a bush unobserved. They fell on him and nearly strangled him while he was searched. Then, empty handed, they went on their way, leaving him temporarily speechless," his throat injured, his voice permanently changed.

The young Petrie got up and—not forgetting to retrieve his wallet—continued his explorations in "that empty land." It is a barren landscape, with red sandstone cliffs and deep gorges and endless sand dunes broken at long intervals by a lone flowering broom tree or sometimes, in the crevice of a boulder, a hardy, sweet-smelling herb.

He had set out to study what he called the "unconsidered trifles" that would remain important to him throughout his career. Sinai's turquoise mines yielded as much knowledge to him as a royal tomb (as would the alabaster quarries of Hatnub and the granite mines of the Hammamat).

As he taught Carter, and as he would write later, after seventy years of digging (the times changed to confirm his ideas, not the other way around): "The observation of the small things had never been attempted. . . . The science of observation, of registration, of recording, was yet unthought of; nothing had a meaning unless it was a sculpture or a treasure."

Nothing escaped his eye in the desert: the ancient graffiti scrawled on cliffs and quarry walls; the wells dug millennia ago; the low stone huts of native slaves (foreign ones were simply worked to death); the signs of the religious life, such as votary steps carved into the mountains, simple altars, or sometimes a complete temple like the one at Serabit el Khadeem.

Scratched on stone, an inscription read: "I traveled here with one thousand men behind me!" The size of an expedition to this land where nature is so hostile revealed a dynasty's strength, its wealth, degree of organization, and the like. The ratio of soldiers to workers, even the chiseling technique on a discarded block, had meaning for Petrie: He could deduce much simply from knowing whether the workers were skilled or only peasants drafted during shommu, the season when the Nile inundated the land.

Crude erotic drawings with holes drilled into the stone told of the soldiers' desperation in the desert outposts. As did "dream books." Left behind in the rubble, the ancient manuals interpreted dreams where men couple, almost unimaginably, with baboons, horses, donkeys, wolves, crocodiles, mice, birds, jerboas, serpents, foreigners, and two women together, all to the accompaniment of rattles and pipes and drums, the instruments themselves sometimes merging with the lovers, with harp strings stretched on phalli.

Here, in the barren land of the quarries, inscriptions on stone recorded jubilant voices raised in self-praise. At a time so remote that Rome was merely a wild forest and Jerusalem an obscure Jebusite threshing floor, they proclaimed: "I hunted gazelles! I hunted lions! I made the name of this mountain famous! Because of me this land had fat bulls and oxen without number!"

"Never happened the like to a servant of the king. . . ."

"In the beginning of my life I was excellent, but at the end no one could surpass me."

"Great was my praise with him [pharaoh]—more than a son, more than a brother. He allowed me to renew my power."

Then there were the rubbish heaps—how Petrie loved them! (Ancient ones, of course.) For they contained the remains of the daily life of the past, pottery especially.

Petrie became known for his work with pottery. It was a passion with him, though he had made many more sensational discoveries: sandals and finger stalls in electrum (an alloy of silver and gold); a uraeus—the pharaoh's protective cobra—fashioned in gold and lapis lazuli; a royal diadem, a circlet of flowers and reeds worked in gold and jewels.

In the western Delta, he had located and "cleared" (of sand and debris) the fortress where the prophet Jeremiah took refuge in Egypt when Jerusalem was destroyed in 587 BC. His find confirmed the biblical text down to a design in its courtyard.

He had uncovered a stela with the first reference to the Jews (now in the Cairo Museum). It is a thirteenth century BC proclamation by Pharaoh Merenptah whose hieroglyphs read: "Israel is destroyed. Its seed is no more. . . ." (On the other side was an even older text.)

In the rubble of Sinai's Serabit el Khadeem he had found a head of Queen Tiye, great royal wife of Amenhotep III and a power in her own right (mentioned in fourteenth century BC foreign correspondence). It was a marvel of its kind, the queen's strong, pouting features and world-weary expression subtly caught in green stone.

He had explored the hitherto sealed burial chambers of pyramids, discovered an unknown script (the Proto-Sinaitic), and dug up entire Roman cemeteries in Middle Egypt. All very well and good, but what was his greatest find? "The key to archaeology," Petrie declared in his trembly, sibylline voice, "is pottery."

Its importance cannot be overestimated, he insisted to anyone who would listen—and Carter listened, never dreaming that before the end of the year, he himself would be searching for clues among broken pots and millennia-old dung heaps under Petrie's guidance.

Carter had come to Egypt to work as a mere copyist. There was no thought of anything more. But now, at the very beginning of his career, Petrie's force and intellectual passion had begun to work on him. His conversation imparted a strange glamour to heaps of rotten cloth and beads and pots.

In this new milieu, these nightly encounters with the excavating crowd, the boy was becoming intoxicated with the intense excitement of archaeology—without realizing where it was leading him, however. "I found him [Petrie] puzzling for me to understand," he noted in his journal. "But obviously a man with both the confidence and the power to solve problems—in archaeological matters, a Sherlock Holmes. . . . But what interested me most was his recognition and love for fine art."

Fine art, though, was beside the point. Throughout his career, Carter sketched, drew, painted—when he was low on cash, he sold his watercolors; but art was not his calling. More important in his life were Petrie's lessons in excavation, the accumulated practical experience of years of digging. He was, as Carter called him, a Sherlock Holmes, down to his magnifying glass and his "snooping"—his analytic method of considering the smallest clues.

Petrie did what nobody else would think of doing with cartonnage, for example (a kind of ancient papier-mâché made from "scrap" papyri; compressed and plastered over, the papyri were then molded into mummy's masks, full-figure casts, and so on). He soaked the cartonnage, separating the layers one by one. The papyri emerged "none the worse for their pasting and plastering"—ancient moments frozen in time. Just one such "soaked" cast yielded a will disinheriting a drunken son; tax bills; scenes of a lost play by Euripides; and a letter by a terrified royal gooseherd confiding that he didn't have enough geese for Ptolemy's upcoming feast.

Petrie would teach Carter the tricks of the trade—how to treat thousands of beads, complex designs sewn onto a cloth that had rotted away (hot beeswax, applied spoonful by spoonful, preserved the beads in place). Or how to reward workers for finds (pay too little and they might simply steal them; pay too much and they might bring in outside things and plant them on the dig).

He would lecture Carter on necessary "shortness of nail and toughness of skin" and on the archaeologist's duty to conserve what he uncovered. He would show him how to move heavy stones; and how to dodge rock slides in unstable tunnels; and the best way of treating corroded silver and bronze. These were the lessons that would be crucial to Carter, not Petrie's casual remarks about fine art, his after-dinner—or, rather, after-sardine—musings about Raphael or Botticelli.

But if Carter was in the dark about his future, Petrie also misjudged him. Even after the two had begun to work together, Petrie delivered the verdict (in his journal): "It is no use to me to work him up as an excavator," adding that Carter's real interests were natural history and art.

Which was often the way with beginnings, as anyone can see who watches "the stealthy convergence of human lots," as the novelist George Eliot so perfectly put it. "A slow preparation of effects from one life on another. . . . Destiny stands by sarcastic with our dramatis personae folded in her hand."

Carter's "cast of characters" so far had been made up of provincial Norfolk farmers and tradesmen (with a few aristocratic "extras" thrown in). But now a new major player must be announced in bold letters: Enter William Flinders Petrie, mentor extraordinaire, arms filled with pots.

A Petrie excavation found him piecing together thousands of potsherds like a huge puzzle. Various factors came into play: how they were made, whether by hand or by wheel, for example; their colors; the materials of which they were composed—Nile mud, sandy, micaceous clay, and so forth. But most important of all, he studied the pot's style, which enabled him to give it an accurate date, thus also dating the site or tomb in which it was found.

Or so he claimed, his critics scoffed, dismissing his theories out of hand and ignoring his evidence, pottery painstakingly collected over the years at remote ancient sites. "Even the British Museum," Petrie wrote to Ms. Edwards, "has practically rejected [his] collections of perfect examples [of pots], all dated." His undramatic though crucial finds were stored away in some back room of the museum—just as later (in 1907) the simple clay pots buried near Tut's then undiscovered tomb were disregarded and stashed away in New York's Metropolitan Museum of Art. (These pots will be written up archaeologically only in 1941.) If Carter immediately understood their significance, "reading" them correctly, it was in no small measure due to Petrie's training.

Foremost among Petrie's critics was Édouard Naville. Scholar, linguist, and clergyman, Naville was also excavating in Egypt at the turn of the century for the Egypt Exploration Society (later Carter will also work under him). He sighed with patronizing pity over Petrie's unhappy pottery obsession, his fatal error, a mind led astray, and so on. Pottery styles varied according to geographic region, not time period, Naville insisted. For good measure, Naville added that Petrie's detailed recording methods were as absurd as "noting all the raisins in a pudding."

But could Naville be objective on any subject connected to Petrie? For Petrie had privately called Naville's excavations lazy, incompetent, expensive, and destructive. Which they certainly were—or rather, to put it more charitably, Naville's talents lay in scholarship and architectural reconstruction, not excavation. An entire papyri library from the time of the Ptolemies, ca. 300 BC, for example, crumbled into useless fragments in Naville's clumsy hands.

Confidentially, Petrie had requested that the Egyptian Exploration Fund deny Naville permission to work on the more important sites. But nothing remained private or confidential in Egypt.

After that, only an angel would support Petrie and agree that pottery styles could be chronological—and the genteel, egoistic Naville was no angel.

In truth, Petrie could sometimes be wrong. He refused to revise his date of the unification of Upper and Lower Egypt, putting it a whole Sothic cycle* too early (1,460 years)—and anyone who tried to contradict him had better be prepared to make a run for it.

He was wrong again about the predynastic Faiyum and Badarian cultures, tracing them incorrectly to the Paleolithic Solutrean. What can you say to such a man? shrugged the offended Naville.

Petrie was stubborn in his opinions and sometimes equally foolish in his economies. It was a capital crime to discard anything on a Petrie dig. Pity the neophyte who threw away an empty tin can after dining on its contents. ("Petrie is silly beyond human endurance!" exclaimed Reverend Chester, a visiting clergyman-antiquarian who was distressed by Carter's appearance. Fortunately, another visitor [a medical man] arrived in time to restore Carter's health with a "prescription" of wine, preserves, and Valentine meat juice.)

But though many charges could be leveled against the father of modern archaeology, when it came to pots Petrie was on the money. For Carter, it was a good introduction to "the fight"—or the vendetta, as Petrie called archaeology. That is to say, the tangle of personal and professional motives was as much a part of turn-of-the-century archaeology as mules or magnetometers.

---

* Every 1,460 years, the star Sirius rises at the same time as the sun at the beginning of the Nile inundation (the Nile's yearly flooding ceased only in modern times with the construction of the Aswan dam). This phenomenon, now confirmed by computer analysis, was observed by the Egyptian priests, who marked the occurrence in their chronicles as a Sothic cycle.

CHAPTER 4

TEMPERAMENTALLY, CARTER WAS SUITED TO THIS ROUGH AND ready milieu of scholarly jealousy and backbiting. Especially as he was an outsider, he saw early on that he would need self-belief and stamina if he was to make his way in the archaeological world.

Both of which qualities he possessed in good measure. When attacked, he gave as good as he got—and there were many attacks. Carter was embroiled in quarrels from his very first assignment until he drew his last breath—and afterward as well. Amid much head shaking, Tut's glass headrest was found among Carter's possessions, along with gold rings and steatite scarabs from the tomb, gold nails from the funeral shrine, and gold rosettes from the pall—Carter's due, less than his due, he would have claimed: mere mementos! If he had been alive, he would not have hesitated to go to court and create an international incident to argue his side. The ancient objects were returned to Egypt in the diplomatic pouch, however, and placed in the Cairo Museum by the indignant King Farouk (himself famous for sticky fingers, royal indignation notwithstanding).

Carter's enemies would make sure that during his lifetime he received no honors in Great Britain and would not be allowed to accept foreign orders, either; after his death, they likewise saw to it that his name would not be found on the Egyptian Museum's grand façade and that there would be no mention of him in the many rooms filled with Tut's treasures. Such slights—and these are just a few of many—are a measure of the long-lasting bitterness that his quarrels engendered.

These "vendettas" consumed Carter. While Petrie could quickly shake off a venomous exchange, forgetting everything in the joy of an intellectual problem, Carter was capable of spending an entire night awake, full of hate. If, as it has been said, archaeologists are "dead men on leave," they certainly lack the calm of the dead (the perspective of eternity) but are goaded on by green-eyed jealousy, vindictiveness, and vanity—with the most eminent often being the least open-minded.

The superstar Heinrich Schliemann, surrounded by a blaze of glory from his discovery of Troy, showed up at a Petrie dig together with a sidekick named Georg Schweinfurth. Petrie enthusiastically described the visit (reported with different emotions by his guests). Schliemann was "short, round headed, round faced, round hatted, great round goggle eyed, dogmatic, but always ready for facts," Petrie recorded. He added that Schweinfurth was "a bronzed bony fellow" and "an infatuated botanist" whom he, Petrie, had thrilled with wreaths of ancient red roses from the tombs.

They lunched. In his distinguished visitor's honor, Petrie hospitably opened one of his precious bottles of citric acid and mixed it with water. Now there would be lemonade to wash down the tinned sardines. (High on the list of Naville's unforgivable sins was having once broken a bottle of the same stored away with Petrie's things in a Cairo warehouse. When the letters between the insincerely contrite Naville and the furious Petrie are unearthed in AD 3000 or 4000, they will undoubtedly lead some future archaeologist to write an essay—"Bitter Ambrosia"—on the high value attached to citric acid in the early twentieth century.)

In any case, as Petrie caroused with his guests, they saw "a procession of gilt mummies coming across the mounds glittering in the sun"—workmen bringing in a new find. The best coffin was Ptolemaic, with a vivid portrait of a gloomy young man surrounded by an olive leaf wreath. Inscribed across his chest in Greek were the words *O Artemidorus, farewell!*

The young man's mummy was inspected, and then the conversation turned to other matters. Poor Artemidorus, after twenty-two hundred years of dwelling in the "world of truth," must now witness, as his first example of modern life, archaeological duplicity.

It was very hot—even for Egypt. "A day," Petrie recorded, "when one thought not of glasses, or jugs, or pails of water, but of nothing short of canals and rivers...."

Nevertheless, as the sun beat down on the living and the dead, the enthusiastic Petrie explained that he had discovered that a pot's style had a life cycle. There was its first appearance, then its "flourishing" or popular phase, and then its "degraded" or simplified stage.

He picked up a handleless pot with two wavy lines painted on its sides. Degraded! he pronounced, for the lines were only a "shorthand" or simplified version of an earlier version in which it had wavy handles. The wavy lines linked it to the earlier version while showing just where in time the pot existed.

Schliemann was profoundly silent. Petrie took the silence for assent and continued. After reaching its final, simplified phase, he explained, the style died or disappeared. "Degradation is followed by death," he intoned as Schweinfurth suggested a descent into the cooler tombs—a suggestion nixed by Petrie, who was in the midst of recording and did not want anything disturbed.

The sun lit up Artemidorus's gilt-and-red plaster coffin as if it burned with the ancient sacred fire—which certainly enveloped the oblivious, discoursing Petrie.

He demonstrated his theory with a variety of other pottery styles. Of special interest were some perfume jars he had recently unearthed. In earlier phases, they were filled with costly unguents, but in the "degraded" (or simplified) phase in which he had found them, they were empty. The scented clay from which they were made, however, gave them away: They were definitely connected to the earlier perfume jar tradition.

Despite the heat, Schweinfurth managed to murmur, "It is certainly very important to know the age of pottery," an innocuous comment that Petrie recorded with pleasure. He was delighted finally to have an understanding audience.

After a style's disappearance, there was still another phase, a kind of resurrection: A new style followed that had similarities to the one that had gone before.

It was too much for Schweinfurth. The suffering botanist burst out that he was "incredulously pleased" by Petrie's explanations.

But the explanations were not yet over! After all, his visitors would surely want to hear about Diospolis Parva (Upper Egypt), where he had uncovered over four thousand graves and determined the burial sequence by using pots found among the grave goods. . . .

He was reminded that the trip to the nearest hotel was a long one (the site was some distance from the Faiyum oasis). But how could that matter to Petrie? He never spared himself and couldn't imagine that anyone would be more interested in comfort than in knowledge. Though his guests were on camels, he himself frequently walked that distance and more on the off chance of discovering something interesting along the way. In any case, he was just coming to the best part: his mathematical calculations!

As the citric acid was passed around, he continued: To order such a vast amount of evidence as is found in four thousand graves (the numbers become even more staggering in the sacred ibis and crocodile cemeteries where burials run into the hundreds of thousands), he used a statistical method known as "seriation." In fact, his brilliant use of mathematics throughout his career has led a modern authority on the subject, David Kendall, to call him "one of the greatest applied mathematicians of the 19th century."

Professor Kendall, though, was judging Petrie "in retrospect" and from the comfort of his study. At the time, the sweating Schweinfurth, his stomach filled with sardines and his heart with a bitterness that not even Petrie's ancient roses could assuage, doubted everything—as did Schliemann. (What Max Planck observes in relation to physics applies equally to archaeology: "A new scientific truth does not triumph by convincing its opponents and making them see the light, but rather because its opponents eventually die, and a new generation grows up that is familiar with it.")

Word of Schliemann's skepticism quickly made the rounds in archaeological circles: a blow to Petrie! Schliemann has stated "in the strongest terms . . . the utter impossibility of establishing anything like a chronology of Egyptian pottery," Naville gloated in a letter to a colleague. "I should have liked Francis Llewellyn Griffith [of the British Museum] to hear him," and so on. And so the conflict raged on, a dividing line—one of many in the archaeological world—being formed on either side of Petrie's cracked pots (pun most certainly intended).

While even Petrie's critics could appreciate his more spectacular finds—the magnificent Ptolemaic coffin, for example, with its sensitive portrait of Artemidorus—Petrie's singularly modern approach was beyond them. His emphasis on knowledge, his "ravings" about potsherds and dung heaps . . . everything, in fact, that made him unique.

▾ ▾ ▾

Such was the nature of the archaeological gossip making the rounds when Carter showed up in Egypt. He listened and observed and silently drew his own conclusions. Foes and friends and false friends chose sides in the battle for truth? For reputation and the best sites? Or for survival—as Carter put it when writing about his own first archaeological dispute, calling it nothing less than "the struggle for existence." The Darwinian phrase was very much in the air at the time and resonated with the driven, do-or-die young man fallen into the midst of this intense and crazy new world.

He was literally just off the boat. A whirlwind had just taken him from the calm of the English countryside to London, then to Alexandria, then to the teeming never-never land of Cairo. He had had no time to pause, to catch his breath and get his bearings. Less than a week earlier, his father had seen him off at what was to be their last meeting. His father called after him with emotion. He paused to hear that now he had permission to smoke. Then he was on his own.

Exhilarated and heartsick, Carter crossed the English Channel and made his way to Marseilles, where he boarded one of the dilapidated old boats belonging to the Messageries Maritime Company. It was still seaworthy, or just barely. His cabin was next to the "smelly dining salon," he noted, where the food was served up "oozy with oil." The weather was rough, and his groans were heard by a fellow passenger. The man, a sympathetic Franciscan, knocked on his cabin door with Christian charity in the practical form of a bottle of wine. His head spinning, his stomach churning, Carter fell asleep to awaken the next day in the port of Alexandria.

Anyone who has found himself alone in the midst of a bustling foreign city knows what it's like to be overwhelmed by a place where everything is strange and new—sounds, smells, sights. But there was no time for Carter to linger in Alexandria. He had to go on to Cairo right away, since it was uncertain when his expedition would be leaving for Beni Hasan. But as he passed through, he got a dreamlike impression of the cosmopolitan city, half Oriental, half European.

Its narrow winding streets were alive with the color of rich fabrics; with mountains of dates and pomegranates and the hard brown dohm fruit; with the cries of street hawkers, splashing fountains, the wail of prayer from mosques, and the chanting of students in the madrassas. The small squares opened onto the broad modern streets, where Arabic mixed with a medley of Italian, Greek, French, and English and where the architecture was French rather than Arabic.

But like a shadow falling over the vibrant oceanside city, there were still signs everywhere of the British bombardment of a decade earlier. Photos of Alexandria in the 1890s show the Street of European Consulates, the Hotel d'Europe, Ramleh Boulevard, the Bazaar, and the Okelle Neuve pockmarked with ruined buildings and shattered monuments. It was a dark chord of warning: Political passions simmered just under the surface.

The Europeans who had seized control of the unstable country naïvely thought of themselves as benevolent. After all, they were reorganizing Egypt's desperate finances and extending its irrigation system; they were building bridges and roads and digging up its antiquities. But they were arrogant, racist, self-seeking infidels, and they were hated. The struggle had just begun that would end in the Egyptian revolution of 1952. Then the magnificent Cairo opera house where *Aida* was first heard, the elegant Shepherd's Hotel, the Fencing Club, and the rococo theaters would go up in flames; the British would be driven out and the British-backed King Farouk would hurry through these same Alexandria streets on his way to exile in Italy.

The young Carter, though, was traveling in the opposite direction: toward the heart of Egypt. Taking the Alexandria–Cairo train south, he passed through countryside that had changed little since the time of the pharaohs. The naked boys on skinny water buffaloes might have ridden out of a frieze in a Sixth Dynasty tomb. As might the irrigation shaduf they turned, the pole-and-bucket arrangement in use a thousand years before King Tut was born. The mud brick pigeon houses still rose in fantastic shapes amid the palms, and brilliant blue lotus blossoms floated timelessly on shimmering, flooded fields.

All his worldly possessions crammed into a trunk and a cloth portmanteau, Arabic grammar in hand, Carter arrived in Cairo. It was a harsher city than Alexandria (then as now): its contrasts more pronounced, its beauties more hidden, its amenities fewer, its climate worse, its past longer and perhaps darker as well, with the ruins of the ancient Egyptian capitals On and Memphis, the sphinx and the pyramids, looming at the "modern" (AD 969) city's edge.

While Alexandria faces outward toward the Mediterranean, Cairo is situated at the culmination of the Nile valley with its enclosed, "claustrophiliac" Egyptian life. For more than six hundred miles to the south, the landscape does not vary. On each side, the Nile is bordered by the fertile land that the river creates. Beyond that there is nothing but cliffs, desert, and tombs.

Carter's stay in Cairo was a short one. He took leave of Petrie never guessing that the two of them would work together before long. Petrie's exhortations echoing in his ears, he set out to join his expedition in Beni Hasan, having barely had time to take in Cairo's sights.

He was formally dressed. If Petrie, even when spruced up for the city, was too impatient to bother about socks, he was secure in his status: He was a gentleman and knew he could afford what amused colleagues called his "gypsy appearance." Carter, though, understood that in his case they would be less forgiving. Throughout his career, he was always meticulous in his appearance, on the sites or off. Photos often show him putting on the Ritz in his homburg and three-piece suit, a silver-topped walking stick under his arm, even while mounted on a donkey. Which was how he was dressed now, minus the silver-topped stick. He looked more like a young English lord than a raw youth setting out to rough it in tombs and burial shafts.

Upon arriving at Minya by train, the seventeen-year-old Carter and a colleague took donkeys the last lap of the journey to Beni Hasan's rock-cut tombs.

"With our luggage and various impedimenta strapped upon donkeys," he recorded in his unpublished memoirs, "we rode through the cultivated fields to the river, crossed over to the east bank in an antiquated ferry-boat, and in the dusk we climbed up the slope of the desert escarpment to the terrace where the rock tombs are situated. And there, as the twilight fell swiftly and silently upon those dun coloured cliffs, my first experience was an aspect of dreary desolation which, I must admit, filled me with distrustful phantoms that sometimes haunt the mind on the eve of an adventure."

It was too dark and he was too weary to examine the tombs he would be working in. But the light of the rising sun provided a revelation as he climbed the high, windswept cliffs to the tombs of the princes and nobles of the first intermediate period (2181–2040 BC).

The light was caught by mirrors placed at the tombs' doorways and reflected into other mirrors set farther back in the dark, cavernous chambers. Here the world of the living was also mirrored in scenes painted on the tombs' walls: Soldiers march out to war, brewers make the strong Egyptian beer, crocodiles laze in the sun, launderers wash clothes, and squatting women give birth.

Birds, animals, and flowers abound. If harvesters gather olives, apes sit in the trees above them, watching. Here a bald-headed old priest sports with naked girls. There a swineherd, milk on his tongue, weans a piglet. Fishermen cast their nets, pottery makers turn their wheels, weavers ply their trade, while nearby idle gamesters play at draughts, mora, thimble ring, and sennet. Bakers and harpists are lit up by the rising sun, as are cooks and singers, wine makers and acrobats, hunters, dancers, butchers, and lovers.

There may have been no treasure in the tombs here, and there may have been no depictions of gods among the scenes. But there were wrestlers—rows of loincloth-clad men covered the east wall of tomb #15. More than a hundred pairs were laid out on a grid like the frames of a film strip. While the men themselves were identical, the twisting, turning arms, legs, and torsos were all drawn in unique positions (like the modern wrestlers photographed in sequence by the French artist Eadweard Muybridge in 1887). The observer's eye swept across the tomb wall from "frame" to "frame," taking in the motion and struggle captured on the thin layer of plaster nearly four millennia ago.

In places, wasps' nests (hard as rock) had damaged the friezes or cracks had appeared from the shifting limestone. In some tombs, early Christians had scrawled crosses over scenes, while in others walls had been blackened by squatters' fires. All kinds of accidents reminded one of the murals' vulnerability. From early morning until late at night (when weak candlelight replaced the mirrored sun), Carter remained "entombed," slaving away like some ancient harried painter with only seventy days to finish his work.*

If he was happy with the assignment, he was dissatisfied— "horrified," to use his expression—by the expedition's copying methods. They were deadening and mechanical, he protested, though he was low man on the totem pole (only a seventeen-year-old assistant archaeological artist, his official title).

"The modus operandi in force [at Beni Hasan]," he wrote, "was to hang large sheets of tracing paper upon the walls, and with a soft pencil trace the scenes upon them. . . . These paintings [tracings] were then to be transported to England, where they could be inked in with a brush . . . often by persons without any knowledge of drawing."

Carter wanted to work freehand, to draw rather than trace. He wanted to show what he could do. "I was young, however, it was my first experience, and in the struggle for existence I had to obey

---

* The time it took to embalm the deceased. Once the embalmers had finished, the funeral took place and the tomb was sealed whether or not the artist was satisfied with his work.

and carry out this method of reproducing those beautiful Egyptian records. . . ."

A few months into the 1892 season, the expedition moved south to El Bersheh. For the first part of the trip, the mode of travel was by foot in order to search for tombs and quarries along the way.

There were four men: Newberry, Carter, Blackden, and Fraser. Newberry, the scholar who had suggested hiring Carter for the expedition, was in charge. Blackden was an archaeological artist, like Carter, but his experience gave him seniority—and as a gentleman, he had a higher social standing.

Finally, there was Fraser, engaged as both surveyor and copyist. An engineer by training, Fraser originally came to Egypt as a member of the elite Department of Irrigation (the official class most privileged because of the country's dependence on their work). Soon after arriving, though, Fraser was bitten by the archaeology bug. He gave up his high-paying job with Irrigation and went to train under Petrie at Hawara and El-Lahun, swimming around among bobbing skulls in the dark, flooded pyramid chambers and subsisting on sardines.

If Newberry and Carter were natural allies, then it was to be expected (on the aforementioned "principle" of archaeological jealousy and ambition) that Fraser and Blackden drew together in shared antipathy for their colleagues. The hot, exhausting journey during which the men discovered only empty, uninscribed, undecorated, and roughly hewn burial chambers did nothing to improve their mood. By the time they reached the town of Sheikh Ibada (where they had to wait for a boat), they were taking tea separately—an ominous sign.

The ruins of Sheikh Ibada, the ancient Antinopolis, were meager. Some marble pillars remained standing amid its mud brick houses, dusty palms brushed up against a broken Roman wall or two—nothing more. When some years before the French novelist Gustave Flaubert passed through, he marveled that the squalid place had once been a thriving city with grand, romantic associations.

For in the second century AD, the story goes, when Emperor Hadrian sailed down the Nile, an Egyptian fortune-teller appeared to him here. He predicted death for Hadrian—unless someone freely agreed to take his place.

Hearing his words, Hadrian's young lover, the beautiful eunuch Antïnous, drowned himself in the Nile, moving Hadrian to decree that a magnificent city with Antïnous's name should rise on the spot—which is how Antinopolis (the City of Antïnous) rose here, where the four down-in-the-dumps archaeologists now sat wearily (and separately) taking their improvised tea. "Bread, water and onions!" as Newberry noted with an exclamation point, silently passing over Hadrian and the tragic Antïnous. After all, there was no percentage in dwelling on either of them: Hadrian's tomb was in Rome, while Antïnous went to a watery grave. The talk of the town centered on the still undiscovered tomb of the heretic pharaoh Akhenaten, said to be somewhere in the vicinity.

Rumor had it that Akhenaten (father of Tut's wife, Princess Ankhesenamun, and of Tut as well) was buried somewhere in the desert surrounding El Bersheh or nearby Amarna, where just now Petrie was raking over the site with a fine-tooth comb.

All kinds of stories were in the air. That Bedouins had stumbled upon the tomb and were secretly selling objects from it—somehow in cahoots with the French director of the Antiquities Service. Or that the Amarna villagers had found the pharaoh's coffin and, not wanting foreigners to seize it, had reburied or burned it in the dead of night (a British officer even claimed to have caught sight of the torchlight reburial procession).

Such rumors were fire, and the young archaeologists, eager to make their mark, were tinder. Carter's task, though, was not to search for Akhenaten's burial place, but to copy the tomb walls before him. And copy them he did, as the weeks stretched into months and the seasons followed one another, bringing changes in the desert that the boy, very alive to natural beauty, recorded on his sketch pad . . . while he dreamed of a discoverer's glory.

Carter's work at El Bersheh (freehand at last!) was excellent, and the Egyptian Exploration Fund was delighted with him. All very gratifying. The discoverer of Akhenaten's tomb, though, would win not only the fund's praise, but that of the world at large.

Is it any wonder that thoughts of the fascinating figure of Akhenaten sometimes came between Carter and the tomb walls he was copying? Evidence of Akhenaten's period was just beginning to come to light in the nineteenth and early twentieth centuries. The pharaohs who came after him damned the "great criminal" (as they called him), striking his name from the royal chronicles and destroying his monuments in an effort to erase all memory of him. Even today, his chaotic seventeen-year reign (the seals on his wine bottles stop at year 17)* is interpreted in a more widely varying and contradictory manner than any other reign in Egyptian history. He is a riddle.

What is undisputed is that Akhenaten, a son of Amenhotep III, came to the throne at a time when the empire was at its height (New Kingdom, 1350 BC). Egypt's boundaries stretched from Syria in the north to Nubia (now the Sudan) in the south. Lesser kingdoms trembled at the name of Egypt. Tribute poured in from Asia; the army was powerful, the granaries bursting, the temples rich and resplendent. But all of this did not interest Amenhotep IV ("Amun is pleased")—or Akhenaten, as he called himself in honor

---

* Wine bottles bore clay seals stamped with vintage dates (sometimes they also had wooden dockets attached to them upon which the vintage date was written along with other information, such as the name of the estates from which they came). Egyptian dates always reverted to year 1 every time a new pharaoh's reign began. Therefore if no wine bottles from Akhenaten's reign were found after year 17, it must be assumed that he had died and that what would have been year 18 had now become year 1 of his son's reign.

of the Aten, the dazzling Sun Disk at the height of day and the object of his constant meditation.

He was deformed—possibly. At least it may be said that he broke with the conventional portrayal of the king. In murals and most especially in a series of enormous nude statues (now in the Egyptian Museum), he had himself depicted as having huge hips, almost female breasts, no genitals, long, "spidery" fingers, an elongated skull, and a strange, gaunt, brooding face.

His haunting features are unlike any seen in the three thousand years of Egyptian royal portraiture. Possibly such statues were "realistic" and the pharaoh was a Marfan's case or a sufferer from Froelich's syndrome.* Just as possibly the portraits were the expression of a new aesthetic linked to the "heretic's" religious philosophy. It is like asking whether El Greco's elongated figures should be traced to severe astigmatism of the artist's eye—or to the Byzantine icon tradition he absorbed in his youth. Or analyzing Gauguin's use of light and shadow in terms of his cataracts. After all the scholarly opinions are studied, one still has to flip a coin—and the answer may very well be both heads and tails.

A visionary, Akhenaten turned away from Egypt's many gods and wrote hymns to the one source of all life, the sun, who warmed all beings from the chick in his egg to the pharaoh on his throne. If Egypt's principal god, the ram-headed Amun (whose name means "Hidden"), was worshipped in temples with dark, enclosed holy of holies, the Aten was the visible sign of divinity that daily crossed the sky. His worship was conducted in open courtyards, standing out under the sky; art of the period represented him with many life-giving hands reaching out to his creatures below.

---

* Two medical conditions that produce deformities similar to those that appear in Akhenaten's portraits—the elongated skull, for example, or the androgyny. However, other symptoms of these medical conditions do not match Akhenaten. Froelich's syndrome produces sterility, for example, and the pharaoh is seen time and again in friezes and statues with one or another of his six daughters.

In an attempt to fit Akhenaten into an earlier tradition, scholars have pointed out that solar worship was present from the very first dynasties. However, Egypt had never seen anything like Akhenaten's fanaticism, his chiseling out of the name of "Amun" in inscriptions and earlier royal cartouches, his closure of the temples of other gods, his turning away from political life and absorption in religious contemplation, which led to the ruination of the empire.

Deserting his ancient capital, Wast (Thebes, Luxor), Akhenaten traveled upriver to where the present-day village of Amarna is located in Middle Egypt. Here, in a completely barren stretch of land, he dedicated the new city of Akhetaten to his god. The other pharaohs of his dynasty (the Eighteenth) were buried far to the south, in the Valley of the Kings. But Akhenaten's vow, inscribed on a series of boundary stelae placed in the surrounding mountains, was to remain here—"in this place"—forever.

These inscriptions, taken together with the fact that his great officials all had tombs in the region, meant that the pharaoh's tomb was certainly hidden in some wadi, some dry riverbed, or perhaps some cliff.

On Christmas Day, Fraser and Blackden headed for the nearby city of Minya to celebrate, while Carter and Newberry set off to search for Akhenaten's tomb, keeping their plan secret from their colleagues. Of course, they were not honor-bound to inform them. However, the detail is important in getting a sense of the mood—an almost feverish rivalry was in the air, Carter's protestations notwithstanding. ("There was not the slightest idea of winning discovery by selfish competition with our colleagues, nor getting the advantage over others. . . ." He was acting "for the advancement of general knowledge.")

But if we can't trust Carter's account of his motives, his description of their exploration provides a good picture of the terrain and distances involved. "There were rumours abroad that the Bedu [Bedouin] had discovered the long lost tomb of Amenophis IV [the Greek form of Amenhotep IV], or Akhenaten, which was be-lieved to be hidden somewhere in the desert hills behind the great plain of El-Amarna, south of Deir [Arabic for the Monastery of] el-Bersheh.

"Encamped on the desert near us between the cultivated fields of Deir el-Nakhleh and the ravine in which we were working, there was a large Bedu family, of the Ababda tribe who dwell in groups and haunt the solitudes of the eastern desert. . . .

"From these nomads we sought information. Whether they had any knowledge of a large tomb in the desert east of El-Amarna. The chief man among them, called Sheikh Eid, professed to know of a place situated on the desert plateau east of a village at El-Amarna, called Haggi Qandil, where there was a deep cutting in the rock, which he described as being much like the chapels [tombs] of El-Bersheh.

"But as the Ababda, who possessed an original language of their own, had exchanged it for bad Arabic, it was very difficult to understand the Sheikh's description of the cutting excepting that it was 'written' (i.e. inscribed). The Sheikh, however, volunteered for a remuneration and the hire of his camels to show us the spot.

"We crossed the desert tract of El-Bersheh, skirted along the base of the perpendicular cliffs of Sheikh Said that reach down to the river bank, whence we gained, at about noon, the great open desert tract of El-Amarna. Here lie the ruins of the city of Akh.en.Aten, bordered by palm groves that grow along the narrow strip of cultivated land beside the river."

Without giving it a second thought at the time, Carter was pass-ing through the place where Tutankhamun (the Living Image of Amun), at that time named Tutankhaten (the Living Image of Aten, the Sun Disk), spent the early years of his life. In the ruins of Akhena-ten's city, Carter would have walked along the same palace paths where the child who would later change his life took his first steps.

CHAPTER 5

ARTER AND NEWBERRY HAD NO TIME TO EXPLORE THE RUINS
just now. The journey they had begun was a long one, and the
guides were urgent: "From there [Amarna] we trailed across
desert tract in a south-easterly direction, our guide obviously following an old beaten track of the Bedu. This path led to an open
spacious valley, situated on the south-eastern corner of the plain,
and which winds away amid the Arabian desert. At the entrance of
this valley, along its bed, we struck the remains of an ancient
Egyptian road. This we followed over undulating ground for
about an hour, when it took a sharp turn to the left (eastward), and
wound up a pass on to the higher desert plateau.

"On this barren boulder bestrewn plateau the track of the ancient road became very distinct. It was swept clear of boulders,
confused masses of broken rocks, and in parts it looked as fresh as
if it had been made quite recently. We continued to follow it over
hill and dale for at least another two hours, until it reached some
extensive mounds of debris, which were obviously refuse dumps
from some ancient excavation.

"Here we dismounted, stiff and tired from the rolling gaits of
the camels. In the midst of these dumps were two deep and extensive cuttings in the rock of the plateau; not the tomb of Amenophis
IV [Akhenaten] but the famous Hatnub quarries, their existence

hitherto unknown save from the records upon the ancient monuments.

"These quarries were cut deep into a stratum of alabaster (calcite) where immense blocks of that material could be procured." The stone was travertine (limestone calcium carbonate), used for embalming tables, canopic jars, temple vessels, and so on. The material for Senwosret I's beautiful chapel in Karnak temple was quarried here; thanks to the stone's pure white and translucent quality, the chapel seems, by moonlight especially, to be an unearthly dream.

"Engraved upon their [the quarries'] vertical sides was a multitude of *inscriptions*," Carter concludes, "*from which we learn* [italics mine] that they were opened during the Old Kingdom [2590 BC]. . . ." And, Carter might have added, the inscriptions continue as late as Roman times, into the third century AD, making the quarry walls a veritable *Who's Who* of ancient Egypt.

"Inscriptions from which we learn," Carter wrote. But just who was reading these inscriptions? Certainly not Carter and Newberry! At the time, they were too discouraged and disappointed by the fact that they had not discovered Akhenaten's tomb to appreciate what they had discovered. They were too hot, tired, and saddle sore to study inscriptions, Old Kingdom or Roman (many written in hieratic to boot, a very difficult script version of the hieroglyphs).

They stood before Quarry P and Quarry R, open, circular pits (two hundred feet across and fifty feet deep), surrounded by huge spoil heaps of travertine chips—and they were brokenhearted. They had hired the camels at an exorbitant price and had forgone the luxury of a Christmas break at Minya, and all for what?

When Arthur Weigall (a young colleague who began training in Egypt at the same time as Carter) explored the porphyry quarries in the south (Gebel Dukhan), he was as content and grateful as Carter would be in King Tut's tomb. He let his imagination wander (as Carter would in Tut's tomb), envisioning the flawless stone floated upriver and then across the ocean to Rome, where "thoughtless implacable men dip their jeweled fingers into the basins of purple porphyry as they reclined in the halls of imperial Rome."

Weigall was filled with awe as he stood in the midst of his desert quarries, describing the "ground strewn with yellow fragments of sandstone, orange coloured ochre, transparent pieces of gypsum, carnelian and alabaster chips and glittering quartz . . . wiggly lines of lizards, footprints of wagtails, vultures, eagles, desert partridges, short jumps of jerboas, padmarks of jackals and foxes, heavier prints of hyenas, and gazelle. . . . Then in the warm perfect stillness there came, at first almost unnoticed, a small black moving mass, creeping over an indefinite hill top. Presently, very quietly, the mass resolved itself into a compact flock of goats. There arose a plaintive bleating and the wail of the goatherd's pipe . . . behind the flock two figures moved, their white garments fluttering in the wind. . . ."

It was a magical place for him. But then, Weigall had not traveled to Gebel Dukhan in pursuit of a royal tomb, and thus he was not disappointed or blinded by ambition.

In a hurry to get back to camp, Carter and Newberry returned to El Bersheh without copying or even noticing most of the Hatnub inscriptions. They left without opening the wonderful "Christmas present" they had been given and returned to punishment.

Their rivals now seized their chance: "Fraser and Blackden returned to El Bersheh the following evening full of the Christmas amenities at Minia. [A sneer characteristic of Carter in "battle" mode.] When we told them of our exploit they seemed somewhat crest-fallen, and did not take it in the light we expected. After a day or so, they disappeared hastily at the break of dawn from the camp, taking with them their servants and tents. We were puzzled to know why. But later, we learnt, from the Bedu, whose camels they had taken, that they had gone with Sheikh Eid to the selfsame Hatnub quarries. And when after five days' absence, they returned, in a somewhat lofty manner informed us that they had succeeded in making a complete survey of the quarries, and had made copies of all the more important inscriptions therein."

Creating a sensation in the archaeological world, Blackden and Fraser published "their" discovery: "Collection of Hieratic Graffiti from the Alabaster Quarries of Hat-Nub"—a "hot" work in more than one sense of the word! There was much hand-wringing and indignation on the part of Carter and Newberry. The latter resigned his post with the Egyptian Exploration Fund in protest and thought of leaving Egypt forever.

While one would imagine that the very graffiti chiseled into the quarry walls, the proud boasts of long forgotten deeds, would remind the feverish archaeologists of the vanity of all human accomplishment, such was not the case. The aggrieved Carter wrote: "In all such archaeological research, there is one recognized unwritten law: the right of first publication being that of the discoverer."

Blackden and Fraser, for their part, claimed to have discovered the inscriptions, arguing that Carter and Newberry did not actually recognize what it was they'd stumbled on—the ancient Hatnub quarries. And so the argument went, for over thirty years. In 1923, Newberry and Fraser were still slinging the archaeological mud in articles and reviews.

Sides were chosen, and Petrie, who had been planning to accept Blackden as an apprentice excavator, backed off, saying that his behavior "leaves a bad taste in the mouth." Which was the most significant result of the whole brouhaha. For Petrie still needed an assistant to help him in the work he had undertaken: a thorough exploration of Akhenaten's ancient capital. Up until this time, the important site had been studied only half a dozen times, all of the expeditions brief and the reports cursory (Jomard in 1798; Burton, 1825; Champollion, 1828, on his way south; then Hay and Wilkenson, both in 1834; and finally—though only for a week—the great German Egyptologist Karl Richard Lepsius visited Amarna in 1842).

Instead of the credit-stealing Blackden, Carter was now pushed forward as a likely candidate to train under Petrie for the coming season in 1893. His careful work in the tombs of Beni Hasan and his paintings of the El Bersheh murals, in the true spirit of Egyptian art, were mentioned. He was also helped by the intervention of his old patron of Didlington Hall, William Tyssen-Amherst, who was anxious to augment his collection by financing the expedition.

Arrangements were made with surprising speed. "In a week's time I was to leave the expedition," Carter wrote later. "In this way began another phase in my career. . . . I must admit that I had sad misgivings regarding this new undertaking [excavating with Petrie] for which I had not the least experience. . . . However, in spite of this, in the morning I arose earlier than usual and set myself to arrange my things and pack." If, as Heraclitus says, character is fate, it was all there from the beginning: Carter's courage, his stubbornness, his truculence, his dedication.

To which list may be added his "demons." For both he and the driven, obsessed Petrie were desperadoes and doubles. But with this difference: Petrie was saved by falling in love—and by being able to fall in love—and what's more, with a woman willing to put up with his Spartan ways and join him in his life's endeavor. Carter would have nothing to console him but his work.

"I resolutely avoided any possible entanglement for it would, I always knew, be almost life and death to me to really care about anyone," Petrie wrote to the young Hilda Urlin in an early, despairing letter. "I drowned my mind in work, and have kept my balance by filling every thought with fresh interests and endeavors, at a cost and a strain which I could hardly live under. . . ."

There was just as much dammed-up passion in Carter as there was in Petrie. But it found expression only in his dark rages. He could never write to another human being as Petrie wrote to Hilda.

"Overwork is a necessity to me, as a narcotic to deaden the mind to the condition of a solitary life," Petrie told her. He offered her no compliments, he made no mention of her long, light hair or her blue eyes (though she was so beautiful that she posed as Dante's Beatrice for the Pre-Raphaelite painter Henry Holiday). Instead, he wooed her with his desperation. "To me life seems such an unsatisfactory experiment in spite of the many advantages that I am blessed with having."

The girl's first reaction was, naturally, to draw back in wonder. Up until these declarations, their relationship had been purely intellectual. First seeing her at a University College London exhibition of his finds, he followed her from room to room, finally managing to strike up a conversation amid his scarabs and pots (whether in their early, flourishing, or degraded stage is not recorded). He invited her to draw his antiquities; he lent her books and sent her tickets to his lectures.

Their relationship deepened. Hopelessly in love, he gave her the key to his scarab cabinet (his idea of a romantic gift). She refused him. He wrote to tell her that he was leaving for the remotest deserts in Syria. She replied that this was rather rash. Her mother invited him to visit the family. He agreed—and the rest was history.

Photos of Hilda and Petrie at the excavation sites reveal marital bliss. Petrie watches as Hilda, wearing her large floppy hat, smock, and daring new "bloomers" (knee length, resembling knickers), climbs into a burial pit or kneels among her husband's pots and coffins.

Weigall provides a more intimate picture of the lovers in a letter to Newberry: "Petrie is a very bad sleeper, and yet for the sake of his health, he finds it necessary to take 'just a second or so's rest' from the hour of 1.30 until about 3.30 [p.m.]. Now during this time the rest of the happy family [his assistants, students, and so on] is making a horrible noise about the courtyard—fitting up pots, copying stelae and so forth. . . . Also the extraordinary sensations in his inside—due of course to tinned peas and salad oil—keep him painfully alive to the existence of a stomach not yet subordinated to the intellect. And moreover the glaring sun streaming into the hut, the heat, the millions of flies, all combine to annoy him. . . . Upon retiring to his hut after his ample meal of, let us say, stale peas, sardine oil, aged bread, and eleven oranges, he proceeds to remove all his garments except a coat and a pair of trousers. . . .

"Next he takes two lumps of plaster of Paris and thrusts them into his ears. . . . Then, seizing a large green tin from off an upper shelf, he anoints his hair, beard and coat with the famous green [insect] powder. . . . The insubordinated stomach alone remains to be dealt with; and so the Prince of Excavators throws himself upon his bed.

"But, stop a moment, I have omitted to mention the system of dealing with excessive light. [He] has fashioned himself a black mask . . . and this he ties over his face. . . . Having now arranged himself upon his bed, his wife steps in to deal with her husband's world-famed stomach . . . lying across the offending portion of his anatomy. . . .

"Going in one day to [his] hut . . . I was horrified to see lying upon the bed a terrible figure curled up, with another equally terrible one lying at right angles above. The face was pitch black, the hair bright green, the beard also green . . . one hand was flung out over the hinder portions of the blue lump lying on its face on the top; the other clasped a stray hand belonging to the said lump. The atmosphere was thick with powder. Half asphyxiated I coughed and horrors! the lumps began to move. It was Professor W. M. Flinders . . . himself!"

In one of his most moving love letters, Petrie wrote to Hilda during their courtship, "I cannot again live as I did before I knew you." But it was just that lonely existence Carter would lead among the desert ruins and tombs.

Thirty years after the young Carter first came to Egypt, he'd finally announce to colleagues that he intended to bring back a companion from England. Which of course caused much speculation about the woman he'd fallen for. Had he, like Petrie, found an ardent beauty to join him on the sites?

Carter returned from leave not with a woman, however, but with a canary—explaining to the astonished men that although Egypt had ornithological wonders aplenty—ibises and hawks and egrets and black-legged spoonbills—sadly, it had no songbirds of its own.

PART THREE

THE WORLD OF NEBKHEPERURE HEKAIUNUSHEMA TUTANKHAMUN

Behold! A reed cut by His Majesty's own hand!

—INSCRIPTION ON A WALKING STICK
FROM THE TOMB OF TUTANKHAMUN

CHAPTER 6

THE ARCHAEOLOGICAL SITE OF AMARNA, FORMERLY THE AN-
cient Akhetaten, is some three hundred miles south of Cairo,
where the desert cliffs come right up against the Nile's eastern
bank for a stretch, plummeting straight down into the water. Then
suddenly they recede in a semicircle or arch, only returning to the
riverbank ten miles downstream.

When Egypt was the mightiest power on earth, in the fourteenth century BC, this remote, desolate spot suddenly became the
new capital. The pharaoh, Akhenaten, had chosen the place not
for political or strategic reasons, but because it was in harmony
with his speculations about the nature of the world. There was a
break in the cliffs here where the sun could be seen rising at dawn;
and this break exactly resembled the hieroglyph for "horizon"—
the moment of the sun's daily rebirth, when it returns from the
land of death, chaos, and night. At pharaoh's command, a city
arose quickly under the "sign"—priests, architects, artists, soldiers, tradesmen, and courtiers suddenly appeared on the barren
plain.

The site was inhabited for only two decades: during Akhenaten's seventeen-year reign and then for the three years his mysterious successor, Smenka'are, was on the throne. At the beginning of
the following reign—Tutankhamun's—Akhetaten was abandoned
and the court returned to Wast (Thebes, Luxor).

In 1892, Carter, mere copyist no longer, debuted as an excavator in Amarna under the direction of the terrible Flinders Petrie. Carter's great "guess"—that Tut's tomb still remained to be discovered—began here, as he immersed himself in this ancient moment in time, making it his own.

The cast of characters at Akhetaten:

Tutankhaten, Living Image of the Aten (later changed to *Tutankhamun,* Living Image of Amun). Son of Akhenaten by the snub-nosed, carefree-looking royal favorite nicknamed Kiya, or "Little Monkey." Though Tutankhamun passed only his childhood at Akhetaten—he was a bit player here, waiting in the wings—its religious, political, and artistic milieu formed him and determined the main events of his reign. It was the world into which he was born. Without understanding Akhenaten's revolution and the reaction against it that followed, one may be dazzled by the beauty and splendor of the objects in Tut's tomb, but one will not understand the tale they tell.

Queen Tiye, mother of Pharaoh Akhenaten and great wife of his father, Amenhotep III. She came to live at Akhetaten during the reign of her son. Tiye was in the tradition of strong women going back to the beginning of her dynasty (the Eighteenth). She followed in the footsteps of Queen Aahmose, for example, who was awarded the golden flies, the medal for military valor; and Queen Hatshepsut, who usurped the throne and ruled alone for thirty years. Tiye was given extraordinary prominence in the records of the time and was a power to be reckoned with in her own right.

During the thirty-eight years of the reign of her husband, Amenhotep, there was peace. No other kingdom dared challenge it. It was unnecessary for Amenhotep III to engage in long military campaigns or to cultivate the martial virtues of ancestors. Instead, he covered Egypt with magnificent temples—and devoted himself to the concubines of his huge harem (on one occasion alone, 316 Mitannian beauties were received into the harem).

The pet names of his favorites, recorded on cosmetic palettes and perfume jars, show him to have been an old voluptuary. However, neither "Little Miss Whiplash" nor any of the other harem ladies presented a challenge to Queen Tiye—they were mere diversions for the debauched king, shown in a late portrait as obese and wearing a woman's gown.

In his perceptive article "Hair Styles and History," Amarna expert Cyril Aldred took up the gender-bending aspect of life at Akhetaten. Describing two Amarna portraits (carved canopic vase stoppers), he remarked, "What may capture our interest in these two heads of royal sisters is the side light they throw upon the character of the age . . . in which members of the royal family exchange each other's clothes, the kings wearing a type of woman's gown and appearing with heavy hips and breasts; and the women-folk wearing their hair cut in a brusque military crop."

Aldred might have added that the women's hairstyle, "the Amarna look," was created by chic court ladies who copied the wigs of the Nubian soldiers—and not even the officers' wigs, but the coarse head coverings of the lowly infantry, who must have caught a princess's eye.

It was a sign of the times. At the beginning of the dynasty, some two hundred years earlier, the preoccupation was with creating a vast empire. For the first time, Egyptians looked beyond the Delta and the narrow Nile valley. Now, however, the players at pharaoh's court—wealthy, secure, and sophisticated—developed a penchant for artistic, philosophical, and sexual experimentation (a situation similar to our own times, in fact, which is perhaps why the era has provided so much food for thought for modern figures ranging from Freud to Philip Glass, who used Amarna texts, verbatim, in his opera *Akhnaten*).

But if Tiye's husband had given himself up to sexual preoccupations, and if her son was now obsessed by God, the queen was interested in politics, remaining an important political influence during both reigns (in fact, we find the king of Mitanni writing to her on Akhenaten's accession to assure continued good Mitannian-Egyptian relations, an unprecedented situation). Her establishment at Akhetaten was a large one—palace, gardens, stables—but her body did not remain there after death.

When Akhetaten was abandoned, her grandson Tutankhamun took her for burial in Thebes, most probably in KV tomb #55. Although when it was discovered, the tomb, pillaged in antiquity, did not contain Tiye's body, a shrine found there indicates that it once had been there. The queen was portrayed on the gilded wood worshipping the Sun Disk together with Akhenaten (luckily, the image was recorded right away, for it soon crumbled to golden dust).

There was another burial in tomb #55 whose identity is much debated. A man in a gorgeously inlaid coffin with an intricate rishi, or feather design. He might be Smenka'are—or he might be Akhenaten, reburied here by his son. The names on the coffin were purposely destroyed in antiquity, and half of his face mask was torn off. But the style of the coffin and the canopic vases (for his viscera) were pure Amarna. And royal. The question of his identity became important to Carter when he started keeping a keen eye on which royals had been found and which had not. The idea that Tutankhamun would have brought both his grandmother Tiye and his father or brother to Thebes would suggest that his own tomb must be somewhere near theirs.

However, through a series of exasperating ancient and modern mischances, everything relating to tomb #55 is problematic. Evidence has been destroyed, crucial pieces of jewelry stolen (by a laboratory assistant), the mummy damaged through rough handling. For a century, Egyptologists, anatomists, dentists, and DNA experts have all offered contrary theories about the royal mummy in the feathered coffin. The trouble began, in fact, from the moment the tomb was discovered. An American obstetrician who happened to be in Luxor was called in and, after examining the mummy, misidentified its sex (one has to be grateful that the young man, whoever he was, was not expecting).

Most probably, Queen Tiye's body was removed from #55 during the next dynasty (the Ramesside era) and hidden together with a cache of other royals in KV tomb #35. She is the mummy called the Elder Lady in this group (again, most probably). Her clutched right hand is raised across her breast in royal position, her expression incredibly striking even in death. After three thousand years, the Elder Lady's face still emanates the strength and dignity of Tiye's statue portraits—leading one Amarna expert to call it "striking, almost beautiful." Her reddish (hennaed?) hair flows down to her shoulders and has been matched with a lock of hair in Tut's tomb—a keepsake found in a miniature gold coffin.

Pharaoh Akhenaten, Servant of the Aten, or Sun Disk. Revolutionary thinker or tyrannical fanatic—or both. Frequently portrayed with exaggeratedly feminine features, with heavy hips and breasts, and sometimes, like his father, in a woman's gown.

The pharaoh's private life: devoted husband of the famous beauty Nefertiti; affectionate images of them with their six daughters are everywhere at Akhetaten. Also gay icon: On the Pase stela (now in Berlin), Akhenaten is seen in loverlike pose with Smenka'are, his son from a minor wife. Smenka'are became co-regent late in the reign, and on inscriptions his name was followed by the epithet "beloved of the king's body."

After Nefertiti's death (around year 12 of the reign), Akhenaten married their eldest daughter, Meritaten, making her great royal wife. Akhenaten's reign lasted seventeen years and was followed by Smenka'are's short reign. During his three years as pharaoh, Smenka'are married Meritaten, his half sister, formerly their father's daughter-wife—making Smenka'are Akhenaten's son, son-in-law, co-regent, and lover all in one, a real-life situation very much like one of the Marquis de Sade's extravagant fantasies.

It should be noted that father-daughter or sister-brother marriages were de rigueur for Egyptian pharaohs and their Greek successors, all the way down to Cleopatra, who was married to her younger brother early on in her career—being gods, they emulated the incestuous gods. However, Akhenaten's relationship with Smenka'are was unique in Egyptian history. Attempts have been made to interpret the Smenka'are figure on the Pase stela as Nefertiti in drag—that is, to identify the co-regent, later Pharaoh Smenka'are, as actually being Nefertiti in male attire and with a new name. But as Amarna expert Cyril Aldred points out, the discovery of a Nefertiti shawabti, or magical funeral figure, in a context preceding Akhenaten's death conclusively disproves such theories: Such shawabti figures were always created after their owner's death. Put simply, Nefertiti could not have succeeded Akhenaten since she predeceased him.

Akhenaten also married his third daughter, Ankhesenpaaten. After his death, she was married to her half brother Tutankhamun, and her name was changed to Ankhesenamun. Portraits of the beautiful young girl in Tut's tomb are made all the more poignant by her spirited struggle to save herself after Tut's death (an exchange of letters written on baked clay recorded the events). However, in the end she was unwillingly married to her maternal grandfather, Ay, and disappeared from sight, most probably murdered.

The pharaoh's spiritual life. Breaking with more than a thousand years of Egyptian belief, Akhenaten's all-consuming idea was that there was only one God. He writes "The Great Hymn to the Aten," a paean of praise to the Sun Disk, the god who brings comfort and joy to all creatures. Its text is to be found on the huge boundary stelae of the new capital (there are some seventeen of them, many discovered by Petrie accompanied by Carter on long desert walks). The poem was suppressed during the reaction against Akhenaten. It was thus lost from the 1300s BC until the AD 1880s, when it broke upon the modern world as a revelation, comparable to the later Hebrew Psalm 104 for its all-embracing religious feeling.

In his wonderful study of Egyptian religious texts, Jan Assman defines the new faith with precision. For Akhenaten, "visible and invisible reality in its entirety is a product of light and time, hence the sun." Assman goes on to "place" Akhenaten in the history of ideas, remarking that "as a thinker, Akhenaten stands at the head of a line of inquiry that was taken up seven hundred years later by the [pre-Socratic] Milesian philosophers of nature with their search for the one, all-informing principle, that ended with the universalist formulas of our own age as embodied in the physics of Einstein and Heisenberg."

Fittingly, the pharaoh took as his motto: To Live in *Truth,* Ankh em *ma'at*—a word carrying the connotation of cosmic equilibrium. To live in ma'at was to sustain the world in the face of ever encroaching chaos and darkness; it was to perform acts of justice, to be in sync with the eternal.

But perhaps to be in sync with the eternal also means to be out of sync with one's contemporaries. For during Akhenaten's seventeen-year reign (1379–1362 BC), Egypt was suddenly turned inside out by royal decrees.

The old gods were no more. Fashioning their statues became not only foolish, but a crime. Their images were chiseled off temple walls and pillars by pharaoh's "enforcers," and we even find them fearfully erased from amulets found in private houses. What need was there to portray divinity? God was in the sky for all to see—the Sun Disk became the sole symbol of the new faith. Its rays ended in hands reaching down to the royal family, offering them the ankh, or life sign—an image that not only is omnipresent at Amarna, but also finds its way into Tut's tomb despite his restoration of the old faith.

It was a remote, abstract symbol compared with the gods the Egyptians had always turned to—the grotesque squat Bes, who helped women through childbirth; or the ram's-headed Amun, who led the country in war; or the cow-eared Hathor, goddess of love. How can the woman in labor, the soldier in battle, the unrequited lover, cry out to an idea?

However, Akhenaten decreed that they must, and the old temples were closed. The images of the gods were no longer carried forth on festival days amid feasting and song. The oracles that explained the inexplicable were likewise silenced. A feeling of foreboding and a sense of apocalypse spread throughout the land. "O Amun," reads a graffito scratched on the cliffs, "how I long to see you once more. . . ."

To fully appreciate the shock all of this caused, one must keep in mind that the function of these temples was different from that of modern houses of worship. They were not meant to serve the populace (who were forbidden access beyond the outer court-yards). Rather, they had been built to honor the gods upon whom existence itself depended.

The Apis or Mnevis or Buchis bulls had always dwelled in their sacred precincts. Divine incarnations, the god-beasts (chosen for their markings) were pampered until death—when they were given elaborate state funerals in many-ton sarcophagi (together with their mothers). Their vast tombs contained generations of the holy animals. In Sobek's shrines, the pools were filled with divine crocodiles glittering with jewels sewn into their tough hides. By night, temple recluses slept by the pools, hoping for prophetic dreams. By day, priests and priestesses danced and sang as the creatures fed on the choicest meats—paid for by pious donations, by state support, and by the fees of temple prostitutes.

In Amun's dark holy of holies, priests washed, anointed,

dressed, and "fed" the images with sacrificial food. Chanting spells and burning incense, they then resealed the chamber, having assured the renewal of creation—more, having participated in it with their service.

As a perceptive contemporary Egyptologist (James Peter Allen) puts it, for the ancient Egyptians the cosmos was "marvelous but vulnerable . . . a bubble of air and light within an otherwise unbroken infinity of dark waters." The sunrises and sunsets, the yearly overflow of the Nile, the growth of the crops, all depended on the temple service performed since time immemorial. Without it, the dispossessed priests of the old order predicted, disaster would follow. And it did, in fact, follow—though perhaps more from human error than divine displeasure.

For while Akhenaten wrote his lyrical poem to the Sun Disk, his Asian provinces fell to the enemy one by one. His vassals sent desperate letters, begging for soldiers:

"Rib Hadda says to his lord, King of all lands: I fall at the feet of my Lord, my Sun, seven times and seven times! Why does the King, my Lord, write to me: Guard! Be on your Guard! With what shall I guard? Who would guard me? . . ."

"Gulba is in danger. The children and wood are all sold to Yarmiata for food. The Khabiri killed Adma, King of Irgate. . . ."

"If this year there are no archers, then all lands will be joined to the 'piru."

"Rib Hadda says: whenever the king of Mittani was at war with your fathers, your fathers did not desert my fathers. Now the sons of 'Abdi-Ashirta, the dog, have taken the cities. . . ."

But the pharaoh had put his army to a better purpose—quarrying stone and raising temples to his great new idea. The empire was crumbling, the irrigation canals were neglected, the old temple bureaucracy upon whom so much depended no longer functioned.

Even if they could somehow know it, Akhenaten's suffering

subjects would not have been consoled by their ruler being first in a line of thought that ends with Einstein! They would have infinitely preferred his "normal" older brother (who died young)—even if his only accomplishment had been to leave behind him, as he did, a tomb for his cat inscribed "MIEU," meaning "Kitty."

When the boy Tutankhamun became pharaoh, the powers behind the throne (the priest Ay and the general Horemheb) presented him as Egypt's savior. A stela (the restoration stela) proclaimed that he had come to redeem the ruined land—which in a pragmatic sense was certainly true. A new era began as Tutankhamun sailed away from his father's phantasmagorical city. The populace followed, taking everything that could be carried and leaving the city to the vultures, jackals, and white ants that devour whatever is made of wood (thresholds, window grilles, doorjambs, lintels, tables, roofing materials—Petrie was severely disappointed by the total lack of everyday implements in the ancient houses).

Once the "great criminal" Akhenaten died, his magnificent city died with him. The enormous palaces that had arisen here overnight were stripped of their fine stone facings. The colossal gilded pillars sparkling with colored glass and faience inlays were carted away. The pavements covered with brilliant mosaics and painted with trompe l'oeil scenes slowly sank beneath the encroaching desert sands. The aviaries, gardens, and zoos were destroyed. The thousands of small stones (talatas) on which intimate royal family scenes were painted were taken downriver to be used as fill in the thick gates (pylons) at Karnak and Hermopolis. The royal statues were shattered. The barracks were deserted, as were the artists' studios, the officials' offices, the royal stables, and the immense open-air temples dedicated to Akhenaten's new god.

All memory of the pharaoh was suppressed. If he was remembered at all, it was in the form of a strange myth passed down to later generations. Like a troubling nightmare, the tale was told of a city of lepers gathered together by a king who sought to see God. And how this king brought years of suffering and desolation to Egypt (a story later writers such as Manetho and Josephus will conflate with that of Moses). Three millennia would pass before the archaeologists arrived to piece together broken jars and fragments of friezes and an equally fragmentary understanding of the truth.

Last, but not least: *Amarna's artists and architects.*

At Amarna, the hitherto unbreakable rules of Egyptian art and architecture were broken—splendidly. A naturalistic spirit suddenly breathed into the friezes, wall paintings, and portrait sculptures.

The creative spirit was freed, and great works were produced. The famous bust of Nefertiti was only one of fifty works of art, many unsurpassed for beauty, found in the atelier of the artist Thutmose—who was well rewarded, if the luxury chariot he drove was any indication. (His name was inscribed on an ivory horse blinder: "praised together with the perfect god, the Chief of Works, the Sculptor Thutmose.")

In a letter from Amarna, Carter described a carved tablet he had just unearthed (now in the Louvre). On one side was a vase filled with fruit and flowers, next to which "Khuenaten [Akhenaten] is seated upon a throne dancing the Queen upon his knee with the two Princesses upon her lap. . . . Petrie says he does not know of anything like it in Egypt. . . ."

And there was nothing like it, or like the other exuberant, sensitive Amarna portraits, especially the king and queen, who in previous reigns had always been depicted in one or another of the traditional poses (smiting the enemies or standing before the gods). At Amarna, however, we see Akhenaten relaxing en famille—the queen dines, holding a duck in her hands; the king embraces his daughters or holds hands with his wife. The young princesses play with pet gazelles or make music or, adorned with jewelry and wearing red nail polish, sit naked by the riverside.

Of course, none of this would have been possible without the pharaoh's sanction. And, in fact, we are told that it is Akhenaten himself who showed the way: "I was one who was instructed by pharaoh," the architect Bek declared in a biographical inscription from a stela, under which he had carved an unsparing, realistic image of himself. Potbellied, flabby breasted, bald, middle-aged, with sunken cheeks, spindly legs, and a worried expression, Bek is no beauty—but his work was marvelously beautiful and new.

Garis Davies, who spent six years recording the Amarna tombs in the early 1900s, wrote in his monumental survey, "The rows of complex columns [papyrus shaped with bud capitals] finishing at the wall in pilasters with cavetto-cornice, and carrying either a simple or a corniced architrave, is an architectural element which, by its harmonious blending of straight lines with curves and of the plain with the broken surface, may bear comparison with features of classical architecture that have become imperishable models"— a judgment that would have gratified Bek.

Finally, there was the huge crowd of extras at Amarna, some fifty thousand of them:

Scribes writing in the new manner Akhenaten decreed to bring the written language closer to the spoken one.

Large numbers of soldiers bivouacked in the center of the city to crush any opposition to the unpopular regime. They could be seen accompanying Akhenaten on the friezes: When the pharaoh rode out, he was always surrounded by his bodyguards. Their outlook posts and patrol paths surrounded the city.

Courtiers raised up from obscurity to ensure their loyalty to the pharaoh who made them.

These, then, were the players at Akhetaten/Amarna. It was a daunting place for the eighteen-year-old Carter to begin his career: rich in disturbing images, inversions, ironies, beauty, and drama—that is, rich in history.

Not to mention a certain tomb that lay hidden in a wild ravine in the eastern desert—empty except for mud and rubble. Given the number 27, it is the tomb of Tutankhamun—his first tomb, that is.

CHAPTER 7

1893
Amarna

WHO WAS THAT YOUNG JUNKY ROLLING A CIGARETTE NEXT to the Great Aten Temple? He looked so pale and exhausted, in another world as he stood there next to the excavation pit. The abysslike ditch got deeper every minute as the sweating, singing workers threw up more and more earth—looking for the past, which, like the truth, was at the bottom of a bottomless well. And the junky became more and more nervous, from time to time shouting out commands in halting Arabic and then stopping to go through the spoil that had already been gone through. First by the reis, the chief of the workers and guards; then by the under-reis, the one-eyed, split-nosed Mohammad; and then by the under-under-reis, Ali Es Suefi Hussein.

But the junky must have been too high to notice this. He pushed aside a basket boy, got on his knees, and went through the upturned earth with his hands, hoping for something more than the rubble and sand that ran through his fingers.

What was wrong with him? He was probably high as a kite, having stumbled on a stash in one or another of the tombs (as sometimes happened). For sure he'd found some high-quality *Balanites aegyptiaca* sycamore seeds among the grave goods of some brother-junky (who'd planned on staying stoned for eternity).

But no, the young guy was not a junky: It was Carter—and so

changed after a month with the slave-driving Petrie that it was hard to recognize him (his first patrons, whose lapdogs he had sketched at Didlington Hall, showed up at Amarna on their luxurious dahabiyya; and as Alicia Tyssen-Amherst noted, they were shocked by his appearance). And though some *Balanites aegyptiaca* sycamore seeds would probably do him good, it was only Turkish tobacco he'd indulged in, the one luxury available to him here. What was more, he'd indulged in it furtively—ready to toss away his cigarette should his boss show up.

For though Carter had now climbed a rung on the ladder of success from "assistant archaeological artist" to excavator; and though he now received a meager salary for the first time since coming to Egypt (fifty English pounds a year)—he realized that his future depended on acquitting himself well at Amarna.

Forget the terrible extravagance of Turkish tobacco, Petrie did not approve even of using a donkey on their long desert treks. Carter had rashly suggested it, as he recorded in his unpublished memoirs (still remembering the awkward moment some thirty years later): "I had to run almost to keep up with Petrie's long quick strides. Once I murmured that a donkey would be useful. My request was received by a dead silence. It temporarily upset the mutual equanimity. But no man is wise at all times, perhaps least of all when he is tired." And the fledgling excavator was very tired! "Excuse my shaky handwriting," he wrote to his Beni Hasan colleague Percy Newberry, "but I have just been out on a walk with Petrie that lasted from 8am to 8pm."

The two formed a curious pair as they roamed the Amarna desert—the older man sparse, athletic, and so ragged and unkempt that the Bedu children taunted him with cries of "Beggar!"; the younger man meticulously dressed and struggling for breath as he tried to spot Akhenaten's boundary stelae amid the barren cliffs. Which was how Carter spent his day off—sometimes. Other Sundays, he scoured the desert alone, at Petrie's request mapping the ancient roads, paths, and tracks where Akhenaten's soldiers had once circled.

The daily grind of excavation, however, was even more strenuous. Standing under a burning sun, he watched through a haze of dust and blinding light as his crew, twenty-two Egyptian men, dug up—nothing. That is, so far. But his luck was bound to change, he was sure of that.

The job required all of Carter's concentration; he couldn't look away for an instant. Because in that instant, Petrie had impressed upon him, it would be easy for a workman, shoveling for hours, to miss a mud seal or to pocket a ring suddenly turned up in the sand—irreplaceable finds. Take a ring offered for sale by a Cairo dealer in the 1920s—stolen during an excavation? forged? The names of Tutankhamun's young widow, Ankhesenamun, and her grandfather Ay were entwined on its bezel, giving us an idea of her fate when Ay seized the throne—if only we could trust it! If only we knew the ring's provenance, the place and manner of its discovery.

Or take a mud seal. In and of itself worthless, it provides an even better example of the way Carter would learn to conjecture, leaping over wide gaps of knowledge on the strength of a guess. It was not only a question of knowing who was buried where and by whom—although as we shall see in a moment, that certainly was very important (if only because the process of elimination would turn Carter's attention to Tut, among those pharaohs not accounted for).

However, the real challenge was for Carter to develop intuition—he defined it in his memoir as "a subtle recognition of the facts." But in archaeology, "the facts" can be understood only together with the desires, fears, and beliefs of an epoch, in this case the end of the Eighteenth Dynasty (Tut was the last in this line). Only a deep understanding of Tut's time, call it "intuition," would have enabled Carter to believe in his quest through seven long years of fruitless digging.

But to return to the nervous young excavator watching over his excavation pit for statues, jewelry—and the above-mentioned clump of mud—that is, the seal of a jar of preserved meat, perhaps; or bee honey, "sweet and of the first class"; or best of all, wine, *nehimaa,* twice excellent.

Its importance was inestimable, whether once or twice excellent. For wine jars almost always were dated (as mentioned, the years numbered from "1" at the time of the pharaoh's accession and continued in sequence until his death). Thirty-eight vintages were attested to for Amenhotep III, Akhenaten's father, while Akhenaten's wine jars ended at year 17.

Let us enter Carter's mind. "In the course of my work [at Amarna], I often perplexed myself with many conjectures," he remembered later—and there will be no better way to understand the young excavator than by "perplexing ourselves" with one of these conjectures, too.

This was the real change that Carter went through here. It was not just that he was digging instead of drawing; what was crucial was that he was beginning to "play" with the evidence he encountered, to imagine and speculate and "perplex himself" with the many possibilities of the finds.

So, let us follow a train of thought that takes as its starting point the figure just given us by the wine jars: Akhenaten's seventeen-year reign. First, we must take these seventeen years together with other evidence (such as the dates at which Akhenaten's six daughters begin to appear on monuments, in the beginning as children and later with sunshade kiosks of their own in which they worship the Aten). The wine jars and the children allow us to arrive at a life span for the pharaoh: Most probably, Akhenaten died in his early thirties.

So far, so good—but typically for archaeology, there is a delay. The next step takes place fifteen years later (the blink of an eye by Egyptian time)—which is when KV tomb #55 is discovered.* Keeping in mind the life span established for Akhenaten (that is, having kept it in mind for fifteen years), we can then rule him out as the unidentified royal mummy in #55. For when tomb #55's young man in the gorgeously inlaid and gilded coffin is examined by the professor of anatomy at the Cairo School of Medicine, Dr. Grafton Elliot Smith, it is found that his epiphyses (or long bones) had not yet fused: one of several anatomical indications that he was in his late teens or early twenties at the time of death.

But can Carter rely on the anatomist's report? Was Smith correct? From the moment Smith performed his autopsy on KV #55's mummy, his pronouncements were questioned; in fact, Smith's successor in Cairo, Dr. Douglas Derry—specialist in mummies, whales, and hermaphrodites—would come up with contrary proofs of his own some forty-two years later. Again typical of the way archaeological deductions proceed, feeling their way forward, step by uncertain step.

---

* To recap: Tomb #55 was the unusual Valley of the Kings tomb in which a hurried reburial took place—actually, a double reburial. Two royals were brought here from Amarna. Presumably, these reburials occurred when Amarna was abandoned by the new pharaoh, Tut, who brought his relatives' mummies back to the traditional burying place.

Queen Tiye, Akhenaten's mother and Tut's grandmother, was one of the burials. The second is more problematic. Who is the young man in the gorgeously inlaid coffin with half the face mask ripped off and its identifying names defaced? That is the question. Could it be Tut's father, Akhenaten? Could it be his father's short-lived successor, Smenka'are, Tut's brother?

At this point, before the discovery of Tut's tomb, if it can be established that Tut reinterred his father, Akhenaten, or his brother, Smenka'are, in tomb #55 in the Valley of the Kings, then it would be likely that Tut's own tomb would be nearby. Which turned out to be the case. Tut's tomb was found a few steps from KV #55.

For a more detailed description of tomb #55, see Queen Tiye in the "cast of characters," chapter 6.

The archaeologist Arthur Weigall (present at #55's opening) was firm in his opinion that the mummy was Akhenaten. He based his opinion on other evidence in the tomb: "magic bricks" inscribed with Akhenaten's name and jewelry adorning the mummy. Besides this, other objections to Smith's anatomical findings were raised: For example, can we be sure that the fusion of the long bones took place at the same age for ancients as it does for moderns? On close scrutiny, every "fact" Carter had to rely on became questionable, which was where intuition came in—knowing what to believe and what to reject.

For the moment, though, let us tentatively stick to the deduction that the young man in tomb #55 is not Akhenaten—if only because he shows none of the physical abnormalities displayed on Akhenaten's colossal statues, the large hips and spindly legs, the breasts and elongated skull, and so on. (Not forgetting that this "proof" might also be objected to: that these statues might be not realistic portraits but simply icons conforming with Akhenaten's new theology. Or that if Akhenaten indeed had such physical traits, they would match a sufferer of Froelich's syndrome—indicating that he was sterile and not the father of six daughters and two sons. The back-and-forth is endless.)

But there is no going forward without a leap of faith. So let us proceed by saying: The youth in the gilded coffin was certainly not Akhenaten (clinging to those unfused long bones of tomb #55's young mummy—and to our wine seals, the evidence that helped us establish Akhenaten's longer life span).

Next: Let us assume that Tutankhamun had his father's body carried to Thebes after Akhetaten was abandoned (there would be no way to ensure its safety at the deserted capital, a remote, uninhabited place; whereas the Theban valley was carefully guarded and patrolled during the Eighteenth Dynasty). So if Akhenaten's body is not in KV #55—clearly a tomb used for reburials from Amarna—then perhaps the tomb where he was reburied still waits to be discovered. Or perhaps, again, it does not: Perhaps in ancient times vengeful priests of the old religion dug up his mummy and destroyed all vestiges of it.

These were the twists and turns that eventually led Carter to Tut. At Amarna, Carter was focused on Akhenaten. He was like a man courting a girl without realizing that the woman he was fated to marry was her sister (Tut), whom he'd passed by unnoticed on the front porch.

And Tut was very much on the "front porch" at Amarna—his presence was almost tangible here, though he had no great monuments or stelae. Carter walked in his footsteps practically from the moment he arrived. Slipping down to the Nile by night, the young excavator started his career ass backward, burying, not digging up treasure: Burrowing out a hole near the river, he hid whatever cash he had on him (on Petrie's advice). The same riverbank where Tut performed a wonder some thirty-three centuries earlier.

For though he was only a child of four or five, Tut had astonished his courtiers by cutting one of the thick reeds that grow here (he could do very little that would not astonish the courtiers). "Behold! A reed cut by His Majesty's own hand!" a scribe had recorded on the reed. Which ended up in Tut's tomb together with a pair of narrow linen gloves he'd worn as a child.

But such mementoes, very human reminders amid the tomb's jewels and gold, were still in his sealed tomb some three hundred miles to the south. The young Carter burying his money by moonlight as of yet did not even know Tut's name (Nebkheperure Hekaiunushema Tutankhamun, for short)—though in the course of his career, Carter not only will discover Tut's tomb, but will become intimately acquainted with all of Tut's ancestors (either discovering or digging in their tombs).

Starting with Akhenaten, Carter will go back seven generations to both tombs of the regnant queen Hatshepsut. At Wadi e 'Táqa e 'Zeide, an isolated, inaccessible desert valley, he will have himself lowered down the sheer face of a steep plunging cliff, where he discovered her first tomb at the ending of a long winding tunnel dug deep in the cliffside.

Using a thirty-two-candlepower engine, he will electrify the tomb of Tut's great-great-grandfather Amenhotep II (the first to be lit up in the Valley of the Kings). Out-Hitchcocking Hitchcock, he will skillfully train the light over the pharaoh's severe face, leaving the rest of the burial chamber in shadows.

Driving through traffic in a taxi, Carter will hold Tut's great-grandfather Thutmosis IV in his arms as he takes the long-haired, ear-pierced pharaoh to be X-rayed at a Cairo hospital.

And as that minor distraction—World War I—rages he will dig up the foundation deposits in the huge hypogeum of Amenhotep III, Tut's grandfather, piecing together fine faience shawabtis, or magical figurines, shattered by grave robbers thousands of years before.

Throughout all his work, the experience Carter received here at Amarna was essential. His steps will be guided by mud seals and broken rings—and the archaeological intuition he was just beginning to develop. "Under his [Petrie's] acute perspicacity my ideas, sometimes very original, generally melted into thin air, especially when he pointed out to me that there was not the slightest foundation for them. Intuition develops slowly . . . and with experience, knowledge also develops. Petrie's training transformed me, I believe, into something of the nature of an investigator, [showing me the way] to dig and examine systematically."

Looking back in this passage from his memoirs, Carter was wry about his "very original" ideas that "melt into thin air," but at the time he was as nervous and tortured by self-doubt as an actor suffering from stage fright.

Which he should have been—for his responsibility was enormous. After only a week of watching Petrie in action, despite his inexperience he was given Akhenaten's Great Aten Temple, while

Petrie took for himself the palace and the center of the ancient city, its offices, barracks, and houses. But what did Carter know about excavating, really? Very little when it came down to it—almost nothing.

It was a situation that would not have been possible at any other time. But Egypt was a "house on fire," in Petrie's words. Its fragile ruins, important clues to the riddle of humanity's past, were being destroyed by natural disasters, thieves, and fellahin. Peasants squatted in the tombs and temples, settling together with their goats and camels among the forgotten gods and the ancient dead.

They used the mummies of their ancestors for firewood, they ravaged the ruins in a search for gold and silver—or simply for se-bakh, the nitrous compound formed by the ruins' rotting mud brick they used as fertilizer. Foreign dealers conducted a brisk trade in patches of friezes and paintings (cut out from tomb walls, provenance purposely disguised)—whatever was stolen disappeared, unrecorded, into private hands; the integrity and significance of the whole was in danger of being lost.

Catching a thief hanging around the edges of the dig at night, Petrie remembered that "one worker held him down while I walloped him. He swore he would go to the Consul; that I had broken his leg. I let him crawl off on hands and knees some way and then, giving a great shout, rushed at him, when he ran off like a hare." Other times the swift-footed Petrie chased the thieves into the desert, jumping over irrigation ditches and canals. "A run of two to four miles is exercise valuable morally and physically," he noted with satisfaction.

The ruins had to be saved and recorded, and the job had to be done quickly. There was no time to be scrupulous about a thief's broken leg—or about Carter's lack of credentials and experience. Working at a speed that would be inconceivable today, Petrie drove himself and his new assistant to the limit.

Carter was very much on his own here. All beginnings are hard, the saying goes, but Carter's was more difficult than most. Petrie was often remote and withdrawn, preoccupied with excavating the huge site. Carter had to build his own dwelling himself, a mud brick house at the edge of the ruins—rough quarters where he slept on palm fronds and was plagued by insects and scorpions. His command of Arabic was not yet good enough to permit him to communicate beyond basics with the workers. Deepening his sense of isolation, he had just received word from England that his father had died, but he had to put off the mourning until after he had made a few discoveries—that was what counted now.

And the discoveries did come. Slowly, it was true, but the main thing was that one by one they emerged from the huge pit (six hundred by four hundred feet and four feet deep), the finds recorded in Carter's precise hand.

Fragment. Neck and shoulders of a figure. Fine limestone
Two hands with offering table
Mauve duck. Faience [nonceramic clay]
Leg, life size. Good stone. Fine work. Dry finish
Magician's bronze serpent
Shoulder, bit of side. Double life size. Good stone. Fine work
Ear
Fragments of the king's face: thick lips, long nose, feminine breasts
Torso of the king. Pure white semi-crystalline limestone
Nefertiti, hands touching, offering flowers to the sun

There were broken glass vessels, imported Aegean pottery, scarabs, bezels of broken faience rings, some bearing royal names—the princess Meritaten, Baketaten, and Neferneferure-*tasherit* (that is, *junior,* to distinguish her from her mother, Nefer-neferuaten-Nefertiti Mery-Waenre).

And there were jars—small ones for eye salve; larger ones

marked honey, oil, and fat. And wine jars by the hundreds; their broken bits came up from the earth, along with their discarded seals—stamped with their day, month, and year.

There were capitals of pillars that supported the temple's courtyard: palm leaf in form, their dazzling two-colored glazes separated by gold ribbing.

Vases were found, false necked, wide necked, and pear shaped. Bowls and jewel boxes. Amulets and whips.

Work stopped the minute there was a find. Carter climbed into the pit and had to judge how to proceed. Sometimes a delicate object would need on-the-spot conservation, without which it would turn to dust. Having the hands of an artist, Carter became known for his light touch (later, a dried floral wreath found on Tut's coffin—a last farewell from his young wife?—survived only because of his care).

The large pieces presented different problems—the heavy, fragmented slab of a frieze with its portrait of Nefertiti on Akhenaten's lap; or the altar table Akhenaten set up at the founding of his new capital. Moving them safely also required a skill he was beginning to acquire—God help him, he could not afford to be clumsy with Petrie just a few ancient blocks away.

The days passed to this rhythm: long periods of watchfulness followed by the sudden excitement of a find; followed in turn by the slow, painstaking process of preservation, recording, packing. Only after hours, or in the early morning before work began, could Carter relax.

Wandering among the desert cliffs, the eighteen-year-old sought the company of a group of beautiful virgins of thirty-three . . . centuries. For the courtiers' tombs at Amarna were almost all virgins (in the archaeological lingo of the day)—that is, although the tombs had superbly chiseled entrances, and sarcophagus slides, and pillared chambers with friezes cut in intaglio on the plastered walls, the burials for which they were intended never occured.

On their walls, Carter could see whole the shattered faces and fragmented torsos he had been digging up. In one tomb, Akhenaten and Nefertiti rode out from the palace in gilded chariots, escorted by priests and courtiers and a heavy military bodyguard. In another, the king in the blue (khepresh) crown sacrificed to the Aten, grimacing as he severed the neck of a duck. The young princesses stood nearby, shaking the rattlelike sistrum during the sacrifice and prayer. And in all of the decorated tombs, the royal couple stood on "the balcony of appearances," showering down golden collars to reward the tomb owners for their service: the steward Ipy #10; the general, Ramose #11; the royal secretary, Any #23; the king's doctor, Pentu #5.

Clever, ambitious men, the courtiers abandoned Akhetaten at the death of the pharaoh, fleeing this doomed place of intellectual speculation and religious fervor. But though they returned three hundred miles south, ordering new tombs and reverting to old beliefs, even in those Theban tombs we can see that a change had taken place. Their tomb paintings displayed the new freedom of artistic expression seen everywhere at Amarna—in statue portraits of Akhenaten and Nefertiti, in the friezes from the Great Aten Temple, and most especially on a magnificent decorated pavement that Petrie uncovered one day.

So enthralled was Petrie with the discovery that from its first moments he sent away the workmen. He insisted on doing everything himself, not allowing even Carter to help.

On its painted tiles birds took flight with a vivid upward rush of motion that made the reeds tremble. Calves frolicked in the high grass and fish leapt from the waters of trompe l'oeil lakes. Amid its profusion of flowers were representations of Egypt's enemies, Libyans, Nubians, and Asiatics, prostrate and bound.

Treading carefully on a specially constructed wooden walkway (that he himself had made), Petrie copied the scenes, though Carter, the better artist, could have produced a finer copy. While

Petrie worked, Carter sat idle for once, listening eagerly to his mentor's ideas.

For it was worthwhile to hear Petrie conjecture, Carter wrote, even about a thistle—the thistle in this case being one drawn by the ancient artist "with admirable freedom of the branching," as Petrie pointed out. He compared it with the lotus plant next to it, drawn "with all the formality of the stiffest Egyptian [style]."

"If one plant was naturally varied, why not the other?" Petrie asked (a question that found its way into Petrie's publication of the pavement in Tell el Amarna in 1894).

"Here the artist's education is seen," Petrie deduced. "The artist had been brought up to draw the stock subject, the lotus, and he could not see it otherwise; whereas on plants to which he had not been trained, such as the thistle, he threw his full attention for copying."

It was typical of Petrie that if he was alive to every ancient nuance, he was also alive to every modern expense. He interrupted himself to mention to Carter a forgotten detail of their arrangements: The price of Carter's monthly ration of canned food and the paraffin lamp he had been given would be deducted from his salary. Then he returned to his all-consuming task—preserving the wonderful pavement.

Despite Petrie's care, however, it was doomed to survive only in his copy. Word spread about the amazing find, and soon the luxurious dahabiyyas of the rich came sailing down from Cairo. The aristocrats trampled through the fields on their way to the site—what were a few pennies' worth of sugarcane to them? Finally, one night a vengeful peasant farmer, sick of the arrogant khawagas, smashed the pavement beyond repair. Only Petrie's copy and a few tiles remain to give us a sense of what once had been.

But still visitors continued to appear, drawn by word of another discovery: the tomb of Akhenaten found in a ravine to the east of the ancient city (a unique orientation—facing the rising, not the setting, sun). The Service des Antiquités' old steamer arrived among the pleasure boats. It brought Professor Archibald Henry Sayce, linguist, Egyptologist, and Assyriologist, who had come to join Petrie and Carter in their first visit to the tomb. For the discovery of the tomb, announced in Cairo, had caught even them by surprise. It was an example of the fiercely competitive politics of the time. It seemed that the French, in cahoots with locals who had been "disposing" of whatever they could sell, had known about the tomb for some years, not letting the British archaeologists in on the secret.

Indignant over French duplicity and cunning, Petrie was nevertheless as eager as a boy to visit the tomb, running ahead of his colleagues to be the first Englishman to descend into it. While Sayce copied its inscriptions, Carter sketched a scene in room gamma: Akhenaten, his wife, Nefertiti, and their entourage weep for their daughter Meketaten, who has just died in childbirth. The mourners pour dust on their heads, while in the background a royal nurse looks on as she holds the child. The scene Carter drew, more than three thousand years old, made first-page news in the *Daily Graphic* of March 23, 1892. A media craze was created over the ancient findings, though Carter privately wrote to a friend that the tomb, greatly vandalized in antiquity, was "a wash"—an opinion that may be considered a case of sour grapes, seeing as how Carter had had his heart set on discovering it since the days of the Hatnub fiasco.

But more important than the tomb from a historical point of view were the eighteen ancient letter-fragments Petrie turned up during Sayce's visit, along with Egyptian/Akkadian word lists, or "dictionaries" (used to translate state documents into Egyptian from Akkadian, the fourteenth century BC language of international diplomacy). They were part of a cache discovered five years before by a peasant woman searching for fertilizer amid the ruins. As she tossed the rotting mud into her cart, she noticed something hard in the earth—more than three hundred baked clay tablets covered in cuneiform, the wedge-shaped script they were written in.

A specialist in cuneiform, Sayce had been working on the letters, difficult to translate because of the diplomatic jargon employed in their writing—words that had gone out of use even in the fourteenth century BC (old Babylonian formulas and logograms from Sumerian, a language that had ceased to be spoken a thousand years before Akhenaten's reign)—not to mention scribal errors, words borrowed from Ugaritic, and unusual Canaanite constructions.

Despite all the linguistic problems, as Sayce read Petrie and Carter his first attempts, the ancient voices miraculously came alive. Taking just one letter—say, the message of Asshurbalit, king of Assyria, to Akhenaten—and putting it together with the colors of Petrie's glazed tiles and the shapes of Carter's fragmented statues; with bits of gilded pillars and inlays from temple walls—a moment from the court at Akhetaten magically came alive.

A letter had arrived in Egypt sometime in the 1370s BC. The men who carried it had crossed plains and rivers. They had navigated the Great Green (the Mediterranean) and finally made the long trip down the Nile. Great Assyrian nobles, they had vied for the honor of bearing their king's message to Egypt's strange new ruler.

Their very un-Egyptian appearance must have caused a stir as they made their way from the quay to the Great Palace: their long, flowing hair, their curled, perfumed beards, and the rich, heavy Assyrian state robes worn on such occasions.

The chief among them had the letter-tablet tied around his neck, its baked clay envelope stamped with the heavy royal seal.

They were kept waiting in the palace's open courtyard. Enormous gilded pillars in the shape of papyrus stalks rose on all sides, their bud capitals opening to the sun that beat down on the Assyrian messengers. They stood amid the gifts accompanying their king's letter: exotic animals and gold vessels filled with perfumes; chariots, horses, and slaves, all duly recorded by pharaoh's scribes.

What the message contained, we do not know. But what happened, now we know from the next letter Asshurbalit sends. Pharaoh had told the messengers to wait, and they obeyed. How long—one day? two? three? We can almost see them standing in the splendid courtyard, surrounded by their rich gifts, as one by one they stagger in their state robes, fall to their knees, and die.

Perplexed and offended, the Assyrian king wrote: "If staying out in the sun means profit for the pharaoh, then let my messenger stand in the sun till he dies. But there must be a profit to the king. Otherwise, why should he die in the sun?"

But this letter was ignored as well; for pharaoh, indifferent to politics, was obsessed by his great discovery—that there was only one God.

As Carter sat eavesdropping on the ancient voices, one wonders whether he was struck by the strangeness of his life. Only a little more than a year before, he was trudging through the English countryside, hustling to earn a living with his sketches of pet parrots and horses and dogs. And now the ancient world surrounded him; its rich fabric of human contradictions had become the subject of his waking hours, his preoccupation, and his passion.

But it was impossible to know Carter's thoughts at this moment. Whatever they were, he kept them to himself. As Petrie later said, looking back on their time together at Amarna, "I little thought how much he would be able to accomplish."

PART FOUR

IN THE VALLEY OF THE KINGS

I've been through the mill—though I'm not the miller's daughter.

—THE DUCHESS OF WINDSOR

CHAPTER 8

1904
Cairo

A S THE SUN SET OVER THE NILE AND THE CALL TO PRAYER WAS heard from a thousand mosques, guests arrived for a dinner party at the British Residence, an elegantly tailored Carter among them. He was older than when we last saw him. His mustache was thicker, his hair thinned, his body filled out, and he was dressed for the part he had been playing for the last few years: chief inspector of the Service des Antiquités for Upper Egypt—that is, he was wearing white gloves and a tasseled fez, the standard turnout for an official of the Ottoman Empire, or "the Sublime Porte," as Turkey was then called.

For confusingly enough, at this time Egypt was an Ottoman province, though in fact the British ruled here. Not directly—nothing was that simple in Egypt. No, British decrees were issued in the name of Egypt's king, or khedive (another anomaly: The title is Persian)—Abbas Hilmi II, who ruled at the pleasure of the Turkish sultan Abdul Hamid.

But if Chief Inspector Carter was thus somehow in the Turkish civil service (as his fez proclaimed), his appointment had been made not by the Egyptian king; and not by the British viceroy; and not by the Turkish sultan or his bankers or eunuch—but by a Frenchman. For in deference to French influence in Egypt, it had been settled that the director of the Service des Antiquités must always be a Frenchman.

Which is *Ummi Dunya Masr* for you—Egypt, Mother of the World, as her children call her. Her history has more twists and turns than one of the khedive's belly dancers. The country's identity is fractured, its memory long, its political processes subtle and indirect—too subtle and too indirect, as it will turn out, for the blunt, politically unsophisticated Carter.

He had achieved much since his apprenticeship with Petrie in 1893, and his hard work and many discoveries earned him the inspectorate of Upper (that is, southern) Egypt, where some of the most important archaeological work in the world was being carried out. But his success had come at a price. His life had been too one-sided; he had descended into those tombs of his for twelve years, to come forth, Lazarus-like, chief inspector at a stylish dinner party, proper and dignified—but with a streak of craziness just under the surface . . . an intense, driven quality that had made him and would soon be his undoing.

But what did it matter? Though disgrace was waiting just around the corner for the white-gloved Carter, though he would lose his position and have to turn in his fez, he had already accomplished more than most in Egypt, leaving his mark in almost every royal tomb in the Valley of the Kings.

He could tell many stories as he dined at the residence, although he didn't, being by nature silent and reticent. Instead he listened to his dinner companion, a young woman who must have been vague about his identity. Enthusiastically, she told him about the discovery of Thutmosis IV's tomb—a "thrilling experience" at which she was present: A pair of white horses were used to drag Thutmosis's chariot from belowground.

To which Carter responded ironically, "Indeed!" as word went round that the cook had just collapsed with cholera (causing the guests to skip straight to dessert, Um Ali from the famous Groppi's).

Irony-proof, Carter's companion went on about her experiences, and for once Carter restrained himself. Perhaps the absurdity of the situation amused rather than offended him. For he had spent much time in Thutmosis's tomb, taking special pains over that same fragile chariot "dragged out by white horses." He had managed to rescue its body intact, preserving the intricate battle scenes molded on its sides.

The tomb was an important one for him. It strengthened his hand, giving him more archaeological authority and reputation; and it taught him to trust his instincts when wandering among the boulders and limestone chips, deciding where to dig. He described its discovery at length in his unfinished autobiography, in one of the fragmentary sketches: "A few eroded steps led down to the entrance doorway partially blocked with stones. We [Carter and his reis] crept under its lintel into a steep descending corridor that penetrated into the heart of the rock. As we slithered down the mass of debris that encumbered this corridor, the stones underfoot rolled with a hollow rumbling sound, echoed, re-echoed, in the depths of the tomb.

"At the end of this corridor we came to a steep flight of steps with a shallow recess on either side. These steps, sixteen in number, led down to another descending corridor which brought us to the brink of a large gaping well [an ancient protective device, common to Eighteenth Dynasty tombs]. We looked down into the dusky space. At the edge of this abyss we waited until our eyes became more accustomed to the dim light of our candles, and then we realized in the gloom that the upper part of the walls of this well were elaborately sculpted and painted. The scenes represented the Pharaoh Thutmosis IV standing before various gods and goddesses of the Netherworld. . . .

"As we stood on the edge of the well we could see the [door] in the opposite wall, wide open. Just as the last dynastic [ancient] tomb robbers had left it. Dangling from it and reaching to the bottom of the well was a stout palm fiber rope which the last intruders employed when they quitted the tomb proper. It had kept this attitude for more than three thousand years."

With rope of their own, they crossed the deep well and made their way through long corridors, finally reaching the pillared burial chamber. However, it was empty. Thutmosis's body was no longer in the tomb, having been removed and hidden elsewhere in the Valley. But a prince remained—rather, his unwrapped mummy remained—a naked boy leaning against the wall, his stomach ripped open by ancient thieves searching for plunder.

Strangely enough, a graffito near the despoiled prince would later become part of the legal battle over Tut's treasures. In black ink, an ancient priest had written that the burial of Thutmosis IV was "renewed" (*whehem*) in year 8 of Horemheb—meaning that robbers had broken into Thutmosis's tomb, which was then set in order, purified, and resealed during Horemheb's reign. Lawyers for both sides in the Tut case, the Egyptian government and the Carnarvon estate, would cite the inscription as they argued a key issue: What constitutes an intact royal tomb? In fact, as the bitter fight over who got what from Tut's tomb heated up, all kinds of ancient evidence and sepulchral analogies were dragged in, though the real issue—Egypt's political reawakening—would decide the matter.

But though that fight was still in the future, its seeds were being sown right now. The signs were there for anyone to see. When in 1899 thirteen royal mummies were discovered in Amenhotep II's tomb, they could not be shipped down the Nile as the earlier DB tomb #320 cache had been. Orders came to keep the mummies in the tomb—where they would remain until some years later. The government understood that just such a spectacle, Egypt's ancient kings in the hands of foreigners, would set off a riot or worse—an outright rebellion like the one in the Sudan.

"Would that Egypt had no antiquities!" exclaimed the exasperated British viceroy, Lord Cromer. However, Egypt did have antiquities, and a stubborn inspector of these antiquities who would soon cause the viceroy some of his worst headaches.

But just now, Carter was oblivious to anything but his tombs. If we are political animals, as Aristotle observed, if the human being who lives alone is either a beast or a god, then Carter was both. Daily he wandered in the desert, exploring what had become his home, the Valley of the Kings, or "the Great Place," as the priests of Amun called it—a barren stretch of land where for five hundred years Egypt's pharaohs were buried together with everything they had loved in this life or might need in the next: their pets and perfumes, their chariots and boats, their leather loincloths and their linen underwear, and, of course, their gold.

The Valley of the Kings is located in the desert, to the west of the Nile. To the east of the river is Egypt's ancient southern capital known as Wast to the Egyptians and Thebes to the Greeks (the "hundred-gated Thebes" had been in existence for more than a thousand years by the time Homer sang of its glory).

Despite the location's fame, by medieval times both splendid Thebes and the mysterious Valley of the Kings were forgotten. The early Christians living in Egypt had no interest in its ancient monuments and tombs; nor did the Arabs who swept into Egypt in AD 642.

A handful of solitary European travelers passed through the region in the 1600s without any idea of the Valley's history. The first to connect the place with its ancient associations was Father Claude Sicard, a French Jesuit priest living in Cairo. In 1707, he made the difficult and dangerous journey south in a quest to collect antiquities at the order of the dauphin. Throughout the century, several other Europeans visited the Valley, recording their impressions of the approximately eleven royal tombs then lying open, some since antiquity.

One can get a sense of how difficult it was for a European to visit the Valley of the Kings from the memoirs of the Scotsman

James Bruce, who attempted to see the tombs in 1768 on his way to Ethiopia. Leaving his boat moored in the Nile and taking along sketching materials, Bruce engaged guides to lead him to the desert valley. The plan was for him to be quickly taken through a few of the tombs' large, rock-cut chambers. But Bruce was entranced by the tomb of Ramesses III and insisted on drawing the blind harpists painted on its walls.

His terrified guides urged him to leave. The longer they stayed, the greater the danger from the bandits and cutthroats inhabiting the desert cliffs. But Bruce stubbornly continued to draw until his guides threw their torches to the ground, giving him the choice between staying in the dark and following them back.

Their urgency was well timed, for word had gotten out that a foreigner was in the tombs. As Bruce mounted his horse, large stones were rolled down toward him from the mountainsides. Defending himself, he wrote that "I took my servant's blunderbuss and discharged it where I heard the howl, and a violent confusion of tongues followed."

He escaped with his marvelous (though inaccurate) drawings of the harpists, which created a sensation in Europe and caused the tomb of Ramesses III (KV #11) to be known forever after as "Bruce's tomb."

With Napoleon's invasion of Egypt in 1799 and the two-year occupation of the French, the Valley of the Kings was visited by the scholars Napoleon had brought along to make a thorough study of the country (resulting in the monumental twenty-one-volume *Description of Egypt*). The Baron de Denon, one of the expedition's artists, accompanied the army south, where he sketched as many as he could of the Valley's tombs. But he had to work almost as hurriedly as Bruce, and under conditions equally dangerous (feeling was strong against the infidel invaders, though the Mamluk regime that Napoleon had swept away was backward, oppressive, and cruel).

After the French occupation was over, foreigners had a better time of it in the Valley. The Albanian adventurer Mohammed Ali, who ruled Egypt in the name of the sultan, counted on Europeans to help him modernize the country, and he saw to it that they were well protected.

Perhaps too well protected, for Mohammed Ali cared so little about the ruins and monuments that he would have quarried the pyramids to build factories if it had been practical (a scheme he actually considered). Foreign consuls shipped colossal statues and boxes of tomb friezes back to Europe, where they found their way into collections such as that of the Louvre or the British Museum. It was only with the creation of the Egyptian Antiquities Service in 1858 that the Valley's tombs began to be protected and preserved and that foreign excavators digging in the Valley found themselves regulated by Egyptian law.

Carter had come to the Valley directly from his work with Petrie at Amarna in 1893—or rather, almost directly, after a few months in the north. But this interlude at Timai al Amdid proved to be irrelevant to him, something of a farce. Almost everything went wrong. It rained incessantly. The excavation permits never got issued. And Carter's co-worker was a young athlete just arrived from England with barbells, a horizontal bar—and a nervous system totally unsuited to life on a lonely, windswept desert mound.

They were supposed to retrieve a Ptolemaic library, but, as Carter remembered, "the rain made it impracticable to extricate anything of the nature of burnt papyri from under masses of mud bricks and earth now sodden with water. This inclement weather terminated in a tempestuous night, the force of which caused our tents to collapse and expose us to the elements, like wet and bedraggled crows. Upon this, my esteemed assistant began to weep profusely. So I hastily packed up. . . ."

To unpack again . . . where? The directors of the Egyptian Exploration Fund hesitated. Petrie had reported that Carter's work had been satisfactory—high praise from such an exacting man. But other candidates had been proposed for the important assignment they considered giving him—candidates who, after all, were gentlemen. For a few months he was employed on minor tasks, sent back and forth between sites in Middle Egypt.

Then the good news came: He had been chosen to assist Édouard Naville at Deir el-Bahri, the site of Hatshepsut's mortuary temple (1490 BC). It was perhaps the most beautiful building in Egypt, certainly the most dramatic in its setting. Three perfectly proportioned terraces, one on top of another, rose against the towering, reddish cliffs surrounding the temple in a semicircle. And just on the other side of these cliffs—an hour's hike over steep footpaths—was the Valley of the Kings.

He arrived in Luxor by the newly introduced "screeching train," as Carter called it in a letter home, admiring the speed with which the trip could be made from Cairo: a single long day's journey rather than the three weeks it would take by *faluka,* or sailboat, sometimes lengthened by contrary winds.

Naville had sent his reis to meet him. In a calèche jingling with little metal hands against the evil eye, they drove through the town with its dusty streets; its shabby buildings and crowded bazaars; its smoke-filled water-pipe cafés, where Carter, unlike his European colleagues, would spend many hours. Here, he listened to the storytellers (even translating some of their tales) and paid close attention to the gossip—often empty rumors, sometimes valuable information, but focused always on one subject: the tombs, the digs, what had been found, and by whom.

The ferry across the Nile here was just beneath the ancient temple that dominated the city; but Carter had no time to visit it since he had to get onto a boat so crowded, it seemed likely to sink. Word had gotten out that Naville's excavation would be a large one, and desperate fellahin had shown up from far and near. The crops had been poor; overirrigation had led to a rise in the water table; there had been locust plagues and pest infestations—one disaster after another had brought them here, looking for work.

Making his way among them, Carter crossed the Nile and then rode out past the Memnon colossi to the desert. The whole area where he had come to live was like a huge Casino of Tombs. Over the years, many treasures had been unearthed here—and for sure, more remained to be discovered. Where? Almost anywhere—"in the innermost recesses," Carter noted, "in clefts and crevices, some [tombs] being cut high up in the rock faces of perpendicular cliffs." It was a place where one could dig for years and find nothing. Or else one could suddenly turn up, at the first lucky swing of a pickax, the burials of hundreds of ancient priests (the Bab el Gasus), together with their grave goods.

Carter's private explorations began here; he wandered in the desert every chance he got, every moment his duties left him a free hour. Over the years, his map became covered with hatched areas that he'd ruled out and circled, possibilities that became fewer and fewer. Nothing was overlooked. A coin minted by Ptolemy III, dropped in antiquity and still lying near a lonely desert path. A drawing at the base of a cliff: a man with his arms raised—an ancient "marker" for a tomb somewhere above? the rough beginnings of a tomb begun and then abandoned—perhaps the unstable shale caused the diggers to move nearby?

He wrote in his journal: "I have marked HC and the date so that any future investigator will know that some attempt has been made to note or copy these tombs, or the places that might contain tombs." Which was exactly what happened some eighty years later: "I saw a shiny vertical line at the precise spot on the wall I was seeking," recalled archaeologist John Romer. "Next to that pencil mark were the initials 'H.C.' and the date. Few tombs escaped his attention. It was not surprising that Carter had been there before me."

But there was no time for such exploration when Carter first showed up at the beginning of 1894. He had been sent here not to look for tombs, but to copy the friezes that covered Hatshepsut's temple—together with the long inscriptions found everywhere, behind doors and across walls and high up along the architraves. This part of the job was perhaps the most difficult. His copies of the rows upon rows of hieroglyphs must be exact if scholars were to rely on them. James Breasted, whose life was spent in such work, forever after suffered blind spells on account of it.

Sitting high up on wooden rigging built by the temple sides, Carter squinted through glaring sun reflecting on white stone, day after day. There were thousands of hieroglyphic images to be recorded, sometimes in their ancient colors, which still remained. After which his copies had to be verified by colleagues or sometimes by Naville himself, who was greatly interested in this aspect of the work.

Because if Naville was a "slovenly" excavator (as Petrie called him), he was meticulous when it came to his scholarship. An expert linguist, he impressed upon Carter that nothing must be left out—a few small strokes could alter a phrase's meaning; a tiny horned serpent or loaf of bread could shift a grammatical mood or indicate gender.

Before this phase of the work began, though, two years went by. The temple Carter saw when he arrived was half-sunk beneath sixty tons of debris. Its blocks were scattered, its chapels were filled with sand, and its rows of Osiride pillars had cracked and fallen. The heavy work of clearing and reconstruction must be carried out before Carter could take up brush and pen.

It was an enormous job—which was why the fellahin had been flocking here, thinking many laborers would be needed. They had not counted on a new invention, though, which reduced the number of men who would be employed—the Decauville (or movable) railroad tracks with open wagons to cart away spoil, railroad ties that could be easily laid down and then quickly taken up again to be replaced in a different direction.

As Carter appeared, riding along the sphinx-lined temple approach, his way was blocked by the crowd of men who had encamped on the dromos. More than a thousand had shown up so far, though there was work for only a hundred. Their shouts echoed in the silent desert as excavation guards tried to send them away, but there was nowhere for them to go. They had shown up here, and here they would remain, their numbers increasing by the day.

For Carter, they were part of the scene, like the cliffs and the ruined temple rising above them. The shouting and shoving, the building violence, didn't intimidate him, now or later, when the inevitable riots broke out. He took the situation as he found it. "He is absolutely fearless . . . ," Emma Andrews wrote in her diary, "carries no arms and rides about quite unattended all hours of the night."

Naville, however, did not have such fortitude. He had asked for soldiers to supplement the usual excavation guards, and he walked through two rows of them as he appeared from his large, luxurious tent to greet his new assistant. A dignified, white-haired man whose perpetually half-closed eyes gave him a supercilious expression, Naville was as different from Petrie as it was possible to be: in his philosophy, in his archaeological interests, in his lifestyle, and in his appearance.

Whereas Petrie was ragged, Naville was dressed impeccably in a dark suit and clerical collar (he was a pastor as well as a scholar). While Petrie's ideas tumbled forth in an almost incomprehensible torrent, Naville spoke in a slow, soft drawl. And if Petrie scampered over excavation mounds like a sure-footed goat, Naville laboriously climbed the terraced temple on Carter's arm, pausing to take snuff.

He pointed out to Carter what must be done. A late Coptic

monastery (fourth century AD) had been built at the end of one of the terraces. The monks had quarried many of its stones from the ancient temple, and the monastery had to be demolished and the stones put back. Retaining walls must be strengthened, chapels must be cleared, and large slabs of frieze must be fitted together.

Some of these, sections from the "Expedition to Punt [Somalia]" series, were already in place. In one, the queen of Punt was depicted, a squat, "steatopygous" figure, to describe her "archaeologically" (that is, Her Majesty had an enormous behind). In the frieze, she stood next to the sweet-smelling myrrh trees she had sent as a gift to Egypt. Just below, in front of the first terrace, the stone-lined pits could still be seen where they were planted thirty-five hundred years before (during his work here, Carter would find some more pieces of the Punt frieze—scenes from the African marshes).

Taking his new assistant through a recently cleared corridor, Naville showed him the secret places where Hatshepsut allowed her architect—and lover—Senenmut to inscribe his name (on the backs of doors opening inward, where it would never be seen). For the queen had showered Senenmut with honors, even granting him a tomb in the Valley. (In the end, though, she denied him the last gift: "eternity." His name was scratched out everywhere in the tomb, while her name remained; he was not someone with whom she chose to spend eternity. After all, she was a queen, while what was he? A commoner—a one-lifetime stand.)

High up on the surrounding cliffs, however, some naughty ancient artist had drawn them naked and making love—a find Naville most emphatically did not take Carter to see.

It was one of the ironies of this first meeting that as the two men walked through the ruins, Petrie was telegraphing the Egyptian Exploration Fund, trying to prevent Naville from being given the site. Much would be lost, Petrie warned, it was nothing less than a crime to put the temple in the hands of such a man.

But Naville had an established international reputation. He had had long experience in Egypt and influence both in Cairo and in Europe. Taking the temple away from him would cause a major rift, the fund's directors knew. Not to mention the loss of financial support—for Naville had written extensively on biblical aspects of Egyptian finds, and such a tie-in was a major draw (an economic fact of life, pure and simple, of turn-of-the-century archaeology).

Caught between the two, Carter was able to divide his loyalty without loss of principle. Though Petrie-trained, he realized there was much he could learn from Naville as well—if not about excavation, then about architectural reconstruction and the linguistic aspects of the inscriptions he was copying. Moreover, once Naville came to trust his assistant, he left Carter in charge for long periods of time and decamped to Cairo, where he spent his time in the khedival library.

For Naville was addicted to his studies, though his writing would lead one to believe the opposite. "I believe that henceforth it is in the soil, in the excavations, that we shall find the solution of important questions which criticism has hitherto sought too exclusively in philological study," he wrote (in *The Discovery of the Book of the Law Under King Josiah: An Egyptian Interpretation of the Biblical Account,* one of many such studies he produced). But even when he was out of his library and near the soil, he did not, like Petrie, get his hands dirty.

As Amelia Edwards ironically wrote to Petrie: "I regret to tell you that though you have been excavating for years, you do not yet know the correct manner. It takes five to do digging in the true (high and mighty) style. At Bubastis, there was Mr. Naville to preside (in his tent, bien entendu) where he probably spent his days in writing to Madame and the children; there was Mr. Macgregor to take photographs; Mr. Goddard to spend American dollars and curl his hair and mustachios; Mr. Griffith to rescue a few small objects and Count D'Hulst to talk Arabic and pay the men."

But if Naville proceeded at a more leisurely pace than Petrie, and in greater comfort, the Decauville railroad wagons kept running, and the mountains of spoil were removed from Hatshepsut's temple day by day—riots or no riots. Over the months and then the years, as Naville came to respect Carter's artwork and reconstruction skills, more and more responsibility was shifted to his shoulders.

"It is certainly quite remarkable how well that difficult work of rebuilding is done by Mr Carter," Naville reported to the Egyptian Exploration Fund. "The whole of the execution . . . has been done admirably. He has a very quick eye for finding the places where the stones belong; besides, as he has a thorough command of Arabic, he can direct and superintend the men, or rather teach them what they are to do."

"I have been able to judge what Mr. Carter can do," he wrote to a colleague once the clearance had proceeded far enough for the copying to begin. "He certainly has much talent. His drawings are very good, and in this respect I do not think we could have a better artist. His copies when reproduced in colour or in black will make very fine plates. . . ." Which they did. When it was published, Carter's many-volumed record of Hatshepsut's temple set a new standard for archaeological art. It was one of his most significant accomplishments in Egypt.

But Carter wanted more—he wanted to excavate. "Due possibly to Petrie's training, [that] was my great desire," he would say later, understating the matter. For it was not simply Petrie's training that spurred him on—he had caught Petrie's digging fever. The beauty of Hatshepsut's temple, the surroundings at Deir el-Bahri, left their impression. He never forgot "the temple setting . . . the delicate sculptured reliefs upon its walls. In those six years," he wrote, "I learnt more of Egyptian art, its serene simplicity, than at any other time or place." But he was haunted by the excitement of excavation.

CHAPTER 9

A S 1900 APPROACHED, THE TURN OF THE CENTURY BROUGHT
Carter a great surprise. The excellence of his work for the
last five years had been noted by Gaston Maspero, director
of the Service des Antiquités. He was requested to join the department as chief inspector for the south, a vast area including the
Sudan (then an Egyptian province). Though his duties included
all kinds of official obligations and administrative work (which
Carter took very seriously), and though there was much work to be
done in the many temples included in his new domain (especially
in the Ramesseum and at Abu Simbel and Edfu, where the ancient
structures needed shoring up), at last he was able to concentrate
on "his" tombs.

For the next four years, from 1900 on, he spent more time underground than in the light of day, working on a long list of tombs,
both royal (Seti II; Amenhotep II; Ramesses I, III, VI, and IX) and
nonroyal (Maihipri, warrior companion of Amenhotep II; Hatshepsut's wet nurse; Sennefer, mayor of Thebes—among others).

Though these tombs were already "opened," some recently,
some since antiquity, the work of thoroughly exploring them demanded everything Carter had—stamina, patience, skill. He would
file many reports about the southern temples, but it was in the
tombs that he really came alive.

Each one had its unique challenge, some requiring a more delicate hand—the murals, reliefs, and fine architectural details were, after all, more than three and a half millennia old. Others called for the sheer strength of will to keep slugging away—tomb KV #20, unidentified when Carter first tackled it, showed him at his best: a fighter "with heart."

"The tomb proved to be 700 feet long . . . ," he remembered. "With the exception of the first portion cleared by former explorers [Denon, 1799; Belzoni, 1823; Lepsius, 1845] almost the entire length was filled to the roof with rubble, most of which had been carried in by water from spates of past centuries.

"The filling was cemented into a hard mass by the action of water. To excavate, it needed heavy pickaxes, and the whole of this rubble had to be carried to the mouth of the tomb by a continuous chain of men. . . . Half way down its corridor the white limestone stratum came to an end, and a stratum of brown shaly [shalelike] rock of uneven fragile nature commenced. It was here when our difficulties began, for the latter stratum of rocks was so bad there was a serious danger of its falling in upon us.

"To add to our troubles the air was also very bad [from centuries' accumulation of bat dung and the like]; candles would not give sufficient light to enable the men to see to work. . . ."

Undeterred, Carter set up an air pump and ran an electric line down to replace the candles that kept flickering out. Sometimes they passed over rubble that had reached up to two feet of the ceiling—crawling on their stomachs as bats fluttered by or the sudden screeching of an eagle-owl they had disturbed shocked them into a moment's pause.

They descended to the lowest depths, reaching the entrance of the burial chamber. Here they discovered that the ceiling had collapsed, filling the room with fallen rock. Digging their way in foot by foot, there, finally, was the prize: A huge stone sarcophagus carved and covered with spells was revealed; one at first, and then a second sarcophagus, both royal, both empty, though inscribed with their owners' names: Hatshepsut and her father, Thutmosis I.

Carter emerged covered with sweat, black dust darkening his face and hands, sick from bad air—and jubilant. For the real prize was the knowledge. The royal names that allowed him to scratch two more rulers off his list. Each such find took him a step closer to Tut, over whose tomb he unknowingly walked almost every day as he performed his duties, sometimes extraordinary, more often routine.

A sample, from the Egyptian Exploration Fund archaeological reports:

> Report, 1901: "Ramesseum. Northeast Wall of 2nd Temple Court, West face of which bears support about to fall."
> Report, 1902: "Tomb #42 Fine yellow mud, now dry, carried in by flood."
> Report 1902–1903: "Kom Ombo Temple. Repairs to the end enclosure wall in progress.
> "The tomb of Merneptah has been completely excavated.
> "Sheik Abd el Qurneh. Mr. Robert Mond [industrial chemist; amateur Egyptologist; patron] has cleared twelve tombs already known.
> "Quft. A naos [shrine] of Nectanebo [last native pharaoh] has been obtained from sebakh-digging [peasants searching for fertilizer]."
> Report, 1903: "Tomb #60. Found: Hairpins. Fragment of alabaster vase. Late, intrusive burial: 4 rough wooden coffins, Christian Coptic; skeleton of a child."

Carter lived alone in a house at the edge of the desert. His pets kept him company; his donkey, San Toy, was so attached to him that startled visitors reported he pushed open the door and came searching through the rooms, braying, until he had found Carter. He had two gazelles, tame enough to eat from his hand. He had a pigeon house and got to know them so well that he recognized the individual sound of their cooing. On a photo he sent to his mother, he noted at the bottom that "the pigeon on the right . . . has a mournful note different from ordinary pigeons."

But the gazelles sickened mysteriously, and Carter buried them under the acacia trees just outside his window. A cobra—which he shot—bit his donkey, and he was left alone with his mournful pigeon and his conjectures.

Sometimes he ferried across the river to Luxor. During the fierce summer heat the town was deserted by Europeans, but that did not disturb Carter, who in any case was a habitué of the Egyptian cafés (his status-conscious colleagues would never allow themselves to be seen in such places). In the summer, the pace of life slowed, especially when the Nile rose and the ancient rhythm of life asserted itself. The high dam at Aswan did not yet exist to check the flood. The waters turned the low-lying desert basins into huge lakes and half covered the temples.

Lying in a small boat, covered up with straw, Carter floated over the desert; he watched and sometimes sketched the great flocks of birds brought here by the inundation. Thousands of pelicans swooped down to fish among the ancient pillars, while jackals and hyenas roamed at the water's edge.

But even during inundation, thieves, dealers, and vandals continued their work. It was Carter's duty to be vigilant, and he was vigilant, whatever the season. The hapless thieves he caught were locked up inside rooms of the Karnak temple, where wine and incense were once stored.

If he was sometimes too zealous, that was his nature. An astonished colleague (Arthur Mace) found him hiding behind a temple portico like a jealous lover, watching and ready to pounce. A little girl had arranged the pieces of a broken jug in front of her. As visitors to the temple approached, she began to cry over her "misfortune." But before they could toss her some coins, Carter jumped out to foil the ploy. Another colleague (Arthur Weigall) told of him chasing a man who had been begging in the ruins. Carter jumped his horse first over a canal and then over a garden hedge in hot pursuit.

But though he could be "rabid," his workmen liked and respected him, even those he had treated harshly. James Breasted recounted that when Carter lost his post, "the reis [chief] of the guards whom Carter had dismissed took him into his house, fed him, gave him money, tided him over until he had painted some pictures to sell. . . ."

Even during the one "big robbery" of Carter's inspectorate— the break-in at Amenhotep II's tomb—the men he prosecuted bore him no ill will. Later, one of the thieves brought him a "tip" leading to the discovery of Amenhotep I's tomb, even though Carter had gone to great lengths to make sure that he was punished.

As soon as Carter heard of the break-in, he had his tomb guards arrested—obviously they were in collusion. He took photographs of footprints near the tomb and matched them with the feet of the suspects. He gave testimony about a gun that was fired, or not fired. Or fired after the fact—the complicated evidence was not worth unraveling, since nothing came of Carter's sleuthing.

The judges understood that the robbery was part of a game, and a very old one at that, with the poverty-stricken pitting their wits against the guardians of vast treasure. Every one of Egypt's ninety pyramids had been robbed in antiquity. If tons of stone had not stopped the ancient thieves, how could the service's tomb gates be expected to?

Furthermore, they knew that the break-in could not have taken place without the entire village's complicity, and they had no wish to put the village on trial (when two years later the British ordered floggings all around in Denshawee, the incident became a nationalist battle cry). Perhaps most important, the court was mindful that just to the south, in the Sudan, the mahdi with his dervish army had not long ago seized Khartoum and slaughtered all the foreigners. Next to such considerations, pharaoh's burial equipment did not weigh heavily. The case was dismissed.

The ill-gotten gains provided a month of feasting. As the smoke of roasted lambs rose from the huts together with the sound of song, Carter grieved for Amenhotep II's lost royal barge and great bow, while in the meantime Egypt's French newspapers attacked him. Insinuating that Carter had worked hand in hand with the thieves, *Le Phare d'Alexandrie* asked: Who is this Inspector of Antiquities? He is little more than an agent for the "rapacious" and "unscrupulous" collector Wallis Budge, keeper of Egyptian antiquities for the British Museum. Why would "a person of no importance" such as Carter be raised to this position? *L'Égypte* asked, pointing to his lack of scholarly background and even the low salary that he had been receiving before his appointment.

It was against this background that in 1904 the service director, Gaston Maspero, decided to switch Carter to the inspectorship of Lower (or northern) Egypt and to bring the northern inspector south. Not as a reproach—Maspero would always be a staunch supporter of Carter's, admiring his dedication and his energy. But he felt that the measure would prevent his inspectors from becoming too entrenched in their domains while providing an invigorating change of scene.

"A change of scene" it turned out to be, but not in the way Maspero had imagined. Before Carter had a chance to settle in to his new responsibilities, the "incident" occurred—or "the affray," as Carter called the brawl that took place—a knock-down, drag-out fight. He was paying a courtesy call on his old mentor, Petrie, who, together with his wife, was excavating in the desert just outside of Cairo. Some other visitors were there as well, Arthur

Weigall among them, a colleague and enemy whose eloquence and social ease always intimidated Carter.

As the sun began to set (it was a late winter afternoon), one of Carter's ghaffirs, or tomb guards, rode up. There was trouble at Saqqara, the man reported, and Carter's presence was urgently needed. Excusing himself, Carter left hurriedly, his ghaffir giving him details along the way. As Carter related in his report:

"About three pm, some fifteen visitors, whom I believe to be French, arrived at the Necropolis of Saqqara in a rowdy condition. . . . They eventually came to the Service's Rest-house (known as Mariette Pasha's House) where they stayed for an hour or so talking in a loud manner and drinking. They afterwards stated a wish to visit the monuments. Upon this, the Ticket Inspector Es Sayid Effendi Mohammed . . . requested the necessary fees. It was not until after some trouble that he was able to collect the money for eleven tickets.

"The whole party then went to the 'Serapeum' [collective burial chambers of the sacred Apis bulls] accompanied by a gaffir, who at the entrance requested to see who had tickets and who had not, knowing that some of the party had not obtained tickets. . . . The party would not wait for this inspector, but rushed at the door [leading to a descending staircase] and forced it open, breaking one of the side catches which held the padlock. Upon their finding, when they entered, themselves in darkness they returned and demanded candles from the gaffir. The gaffir explained to them that he had not any candles nor did the Service supply visitors with candles. The party then roughly handled the gaffir and demanded their money back. . . ."

It was fitting that the fight began at the Serapeum, where for century after century the animal-gods were buried. Though the French visitors did not descend into its endless corridors, the psychic energy of the gloomy labyrinth worked on them—at least in the opinion of the clairvoyant gossips, the mediums who held court at Cairo's soirees. For the Serapeum was a place of magic and spiritual energy. So much so that the Ramesside prince Khaemwaset—a famed adept in the esoteric arts—chose to be ritually buried here.

Whatever one believed, one fact was certain: The excited French party was clearly under the influence of spirits—either bottled, as Carter claimed, or buried, as the mediums asserted. Shouting and shoving the ghaffir, they returned to the service rest house, where they barricaded the doors and tried by force to get back their entrance fees.

When he arrived, Carter had difficulty entering the house, where the drunken visitors were becoming more and more unreasonable. As his report recounted: "On finding one of them knew English I requested him to give an explanation. He and all of them spoke to me in an exceedingly rough way and I was unable to get from them a proper explanation. I then requested the above Inspector to explain what had occurred, and he told me how they had entered the 'Serapeum' by force and of their general behavior.

"I then explained to them that they had no right to take such steps or touch the men and that they had no right to be in the house, it being private property, and that they must leave it at once. This they refused to do. I told them that if they did not go out steps would have to be taken to remove them and at the same time I requested their names.

"They . . . became more offensive. On my again warning them, and on my telling the gaffirs that the party must be turned out, one of the party immediately without any reason struck a gaffir with his fist in the face and knocked him down in a savage manner. On my interfering the same man raised his hand and threatened to strike me. I arrested his striking arm and warned him. The number of gaffirs . . . being inadequate to remove these people, I commanded Reis Khalifa to send for more and on their entering by the second door the whole of the [French] party immediately attacked them with their sticks and chairs belonging to the Service.

"Seeing that the gaffirs were being very badly knocked about I at once gave them the order to defend themselves and drive the people out. In the affray some of the party were hit, one of them being knocked down. The party fled leaving one injured man which I attended to and during the meantime one of the party returned. From outside stones were hurled at us. . . . I wish to commend the gaffirs on their behavior during the whole affray.

"Upon the arrival of the police a complete enquiry and procès verbal was made, consisting of some 35 sheets of foolscap.

"I beg to request that legal steps should be taken against these people for assaulting the gaffirs, in raising a hand with intent to attack me, and for damaging Government property. Howard Carter."

Carter not only wrote on foolscap, though, but wore one as he pursued "justice." He telegraphed a shorter version of his report to the British viceroy, Lord Cromer. "My Lord, I am exceedingly sorry to inform you that a bad affray has occurred. . . ."

More important than the text, as it turned out, was its context. Carter had only to look above or below the lines he was writing to see what the outcome of the case would be.

The telegram's top: "Administration des Télégraphes."

Its bottom:

Les indication au dessou de cette ligne ne sont transmises que sur la demande expresse de l'Expéditeur

Signature de l'Expéditeur. . . .

That is, a mere glance at the telegraph form should have reminded Carter of France's influence in Egypt, strong enough to make French the second language. In addition, any newspaper he picked up would have made some mention of the Entente cordiale, then barely a year old. Great Britain and France were drawing together as World War I approached; the powers that would fight together had begun to choose sides. Carter must have realized that the rowdy Frenchmen would complain to their consul. And if he thought that Cromer would back him, it was because he understood nothing of the political balancing act that went on every day in Egypt.

In their complaint, the French stated that Carter ordered his guards "to drive away these dirty French and to strike them . . ."; and that one man was struck with a stone and fell "bathed in blood," while another man's forehead was cut open by a stick. The French consul asked Lord Cromer to "draw the conclusion of such an act ordered by an English official. . . ." For in such a case as this, Carter was identified with the English, his Turkish fez notwithstanding.

A Justice Department commission investigated and vindicated Carter—which meant nothing to the British viceroy. Carter recorded that during his interview with him, "Lord Cromer said that he considered I was entirely in the wrong, that I could have prevented the affair when I saw the people were excited instead of aggravating it. To set natives against Europeans was not a proper thing to do, that he agreed with Sir William Garstin [an official who severely reprimanded Carter], and that he can have nothing more to do with the matter."

How could Carter have been such a babe in arms? Did he really believe Cromer would permit Egyptians to strike Europeans, whatever the provocation?

If they beat the French today, tomorrow the British would be in danger. Besides which, Europeans were civilized while Egyptians were dirty, dishonest, unscrupulous, inferior, savage, sensual, half-naked, fatalistic, lazy, unambitious, shifty, and scheming—so went the old song.

Even Arthur Weigall, supposedly liberal, wrote in his description of Lord Cromer, "In no disparaging sense it may be said that he did not trouble himself to understand the Egyptian mind. . . . He never learnt to speak Arabic [though Cromer was fluent in Turkish, French, Greek, and Latin] and he made no effort to adapt his manners to the habit of the land. When he retired he knew as little of Egyptian thought as he did of Arabic grammar." Weigall's phrase "in no disparaging sense" said it all—the assumption was that a British viceroy need not take the trouble to understand these "sensual . . . scheming" people over whom he ruled.

Only Petrie lauded Carter's action (both at the time and later in his memoirs). But Petrie's attitude was exceptional. Like Carter, Petrie admired the Egyptians; and like Carter, he lived with his workers on the closest terms. Both men were protective of their helpers, sending them out of unstable tunnels while remaining themselves to dodge rock slides. And both men were more attuned to life in the villages than they were to sophisticated London or Cairo.

But while Carter did not reflect on the situation in general or on his own attitude—it was second nature to him—Petrie was more self-conscious and thoughtful. When Petrie praised the Egyptians, as he often did in his writings and lectures, his praise contained an implied criticism of his fellow archaeologists: "They [the Egyptian workers] had dry bread to eat and brackish water to drink. . . . They toiled for sixpence a day . . . and they had to walk twenty-five to forty miles to get food. For shelter, they dug holes in sand mounds or made booths with tamarisk bushes. . . .

"Each night a blazing row of camp fires flickered their yellow flames up into the starlight all along the line of booths. . . . The boys playing games in dark starlight, the girls singing and clapping hands . . . and not another sound, nothing but sand and tamarisks and marsh and water and desolation.

"But I liked it better than most civilized places; one lives with the people more and the ever fresh desert air, doubles one's contentment and peace of mind. Neither [the linguist] Gardiner nor Griffith [of the British Museum] would appreciate it, I fear; they neither of them like having to do with the people and would prefer an immense excavating machine to do their work. To me, all their [the Egyptians'] by-play and jokes and songs and ways give a color and an interest to life here which no one will ever reach in staid, school boarded England."

But it was one thing to admire the Egyptians, and it was another to order your workers to beat up some drunken Frenchmen. And while that was bad enough, what made it worse, inexcusable, was that Carter insisted he was right.

On Cromer's orders, Sir William Garstin, legal adviser to the Department of Public Works, instructed Carter to apologize. Carter refused. Maspero tried to smooth things over—what was really required, he told Carter in his suave way, was not an apology but an expression of regret for what happened. Surely Carter regretted the "affray"?

Carter did, or felt obliged to say he did. But he still insisted that any expression of regret must be accompanied by the other side's expression of regret.

Maspero wrote to Carter: "You are to come with me tomorrow between nine and ten and pay a call on M. de la Boulinière [the French consul] there to express our regrets that the order you gave brought so strong consequences. That will stop the matter which is becoming irritating."

Carter answered Maspero: "I feel the humiliation to an exceeding extent. The treatment I have received after I have carried out my duty which has always been my endeavor and after my services to the Department [of Antiquities] is inconceivable."

Theodore Davis (the American millionaire patron of Egyptology) wrote to Carter: "Pay no attention to whatever the papers or vain and silly people may say! All men whose respect is worth having will praise and approve of your action. Contemplate the harm of being dismissed from the service 'for disobedience.' It will stick to you as long as you live, and all your justification will be forgotten."

Carter to Davis: "I cannot believe that they will allow a gentleman to be treated in such a way while endeavoring to carry out his duty." And so forth.

Davis to Carter a long emotional letter: "I received your letter and have in sadness and thoughtfulness considered your attitude. You are so entirely wrong, and in danger of a crushing blow. The row at Sakkara was submitted to a [Department of Justice] Commission and you were held to be justified in your activities even if you used 'a high hand.' Now comes your trouble. The French minister asked the Government to desire you (or rather to desire the Inspector general) to apologize for the connection the Inspector General had with the Sakkara row.

"It seems that the government concluded that whatever might be the rights and wrongs of the affair, it would be a wise and friendly thing to do as between the two Governments, particularly as the French minister stated that he wanted only an expression of regret of the affair, a shake of the hand etc.

"Thereupon you were directed or requested to go through the form as above stated. This you refused to do, in spite of astounding fatherly advice of M. Maspero and Sir William [Garstin].

"I have as per your letter your reasons are:

"1st 'I have no doubt that the instant that I went to the French embassy the papers would publish at once.' The natural deductions from this, and certainly that of the public, would be, that thereby your pride, vanity, or self love would be wounded. Can you for a moment lay yourself open to such attribution?

"2nd 'My offer has been that if these people will apologize to my Director, then I will take the step of responding etc.' "

Davis concluded with a statement that summed up the opinion of European Cairo (Petrie excepted): "There is only one upright and gentlemanly thing to do etc."—that is, apologize!

But Carter could not. Some months went by, and at the beginning of the summer of 1905 he was banished farther north, to

Tanta in the Delta, to take up a position of reduced responsibility. To make matters worse, Arthur Weigall was appointed chief inspector in his place.

Dispirited, physically sick from the strain, Carter arrived in Tanta among thousands of pilgrims—it was the moulid, or birthday of the dead saint El-Sayyed el Bedawi, buried at the city's edge. Maspero, sensing that Carter was about to resign, had repeatedly implored him to put his work first, not to let his pride get the better of him, to stay at his post and do his duty.

But again, Carter could not. To the sound of the pilgrims' revelry and prayer, he wrote Maspero asking for three months' leave. Maspero arranged it, and Carter traveled to England, where he visited the scenes of his youth. But when he returned to take up his post in Tanta, he was just as unhappy as before: His heart was not in it. After a few months of trying to throw himself into his work, he finally wrote a letter of resignation.

He had lost the inspectorate it had taken him twelve years to gain. With no immediate prospects in sight, he returned to Cairo.

It would take another decade of backbreaking work for him to triumph over his critics. But at that moment of triumph, when he discovered Tut's tomb, he would make the same mistakes all over again. He would act without discretion, he would allow his dark feelings to get the upper hand, he would ignore political realities— and again disaster followed, this time magnified times ten.

He would be locked out of Tut's tomb for two years by the authorities. All work ceased; the doors were resealed, though Carter had been in the midst of crucial work, raising the heavy stone sarcophagus cover with rope and tackle—with Tut lying just beneath, within three nested coffins. This, while the enraged Carter spent his days writing angry letters, issuing self-justifying pamphlets, consulting with lawyers, badgering British officials, and snarling at newspaper reporters—among whom was Arthur Weigall. For after a nervous breakdown, Weigall had turned to writing to make a living (his malicious articles about Carter brought him hefty fees).

Watching the spectacle even from this distance in time, one wants to cry out: No! Stop it! Control yourself, Carter! But the truth of the matter is that Carter could not control himself. For though he was remarkable, he was also a little—more than a little—crazy. You couldn't be Howard Carter and not be. The same driven quality that enabled him to find Tut's tomb also brought about his downfall.

Weigall privately circulated a caricature he'd drawn of Carter looking very much like Charlie Chaplin. In the sketch a ragged Carter hit the road, following a sign advertising cheap lodgings. Weigall especially had little sympathy for the ex–chief inspector: Carter had brought the Saqqara trouble upon himself, Weigall wrote to his wife, the man was filled with childish pride, vanity, and stubbornness.

Say Weigall was right, Carter's flawed character had led him to resign—his pride, vanity, and anger. Or say Carter was right, that a strong sense of principle and ethical disgust made him throw in the towel. Or—probably the case—say both were right: In the end it came to the same thing. The strong flow of Carter's feelings, the intensity that made him abandon his post at the service, was also what led him to make the greatest discovery in the history of Egyptology . . . perhaps a bad moral with which to conclude, but an interesting reflection on our human nature.

Right or wrong, Carter was suffering, alone and without a penny, after his resignation. But the insult he had received only fueled his determination. He might be down in Cairo—but he was not down and out.

One Month Later

Cairo was a city of refuge for outcasts. It was blind to faults, forgiving of sins, delighted by scandal. When Lady Atherton, for example, was exposed as an adulteress by her French maid, where did she go? She left the terribly straitlaced London and came to Cairo, of course, where the new inspector of antiquities—Arthur Weigall—squired her around. Or, to take another example, when Prince Oblonsky lost everything at the Baden-Baden casino, where was he next seen? In Cairo, naturally, where he was all but applauded for his prodigality.

Even that supposedly virtuous dame the Statue of Liberty planned on taking up residence here. (Her original name was *An Allegory of Egypt Holding Out the Light of Learning to Asia.* She was intended as a gift from the people of France to Egypt.) But King Isma'il of Egypt was going bankrupt and didn't have the dough to bring her over from France. Otherwise she might have been the Statue of License, not Liberty, and her inscription would have proclaimed: "Give me your spendthrifts! Your lustful! Your social outcasts yearning to be free!"

Only one outcast was beyond the pale—the unrepentant Carter. After resigning as chief inspector, he was cold-shouldered by the elite and blacklisted as an excavator. It was not official, of course, but for the next three years, all doors were shut. Nothing could open them—neither Maspero's affection for him, nor the efforts of Percy Newberry, his old Beni Hasan colleague, nor his brilliant record as inspector. He had ordered Egyptians to beat Europeans. ("That is the really bad part of the business," Maspero wrote to Carter in an off-the-record letter. "Native policemen ought to let themselves be struck without striking back.") No, Carter had proved himself not to be a gentleman. He was all washed up.

The only reasonable course of action, he knew, would have been to beg, borrow, or steal the return fare to England. But instead, Carter used whatever money he had to head south, to the Valley of the Kings. When he got off the train at Luxor in 1905, he had no place to live, no money, and no idea whether he would be able to support himself.

The American Egyptologist James Breasted reported firsthand (and Breasted's son has confirmed) that Carter went to live in the hut of an Egyptian tomb guard whom he had fired. He ate at the man's table and even borrowed money from him. What Carter's fellow Europeans thought about this arrangement may be easily guessed. But Carter did not care. He was determined to find a way of remaining in the Valley and quickly settled into a routine, spending his nights in the hut at Gurneh (the desert's edge) and emerging each morning to paint the ruins.

The ex–chief inspector at his easel—what an astonishing sight it must have been for the beggars, urchins, and thieves he had driven away. Now they were thrown not into the Karnak temple jail, but into Carter's paintings, where they were used to create local color—a child playing at the entrance of a tomb, a beggar stretching out his hand under a crumbling arch. It was not great art, but it was salable, that was the main thing: It appealed to all sorts of people passing through Luxor and helped Carter keep body and soul together.

He developed other sidelines as well. He became a familiar figure at the ruins, taking around visitors who wanted a deeper understanding of their history. He was to be seen in the bazaars, offering his expertise to those who were interested in purchasing antiquities but were afraid of ending up with one of Oxan Aslanian's "masterpieces" (the great Berlin forger was working in Egypt during this time).

Now and then, the thieves themselves helped Carter to earn a commission. We find him approaching the American millionaire Theodore Davis on their behalf (at that time Davis was digging, or rather bankrolling the archaeologist Edward Ayrton to dig, in the Valley, unmethodically, striking out in all directions for whatever they might find). Carter offered Davis a hoard of small precious objects, jewelry and scarabs, all stolen from his dig. For a fair price, they would be returned—no questions asked, no arrests made. It was a mark of the thieves' respect for Carter that they had made him their emissary—and a thief's respect is worth having, especially in the antiquities game.

With such makeshift stratagems as these, Carter managed to survive while, unknown to him, the man who would be his future partner arrived in Cairo. And in style—the Earl and Countess of Carnarvon took a suite at Shepherd's, where they prepared to remain for the 1905 season—or so the *Egyptian Gazette* reported.

It was not long, though, before Carnarvon tired of the social round and thought it might be just the thing to try his hand at some excavating. He took up the idea lightly. And though as time went on he pursued it with increasing seriousness, it never became the desperate obsession for him that it was for Carter. He never went slithering over mounds of debris in unstable tomb corridors or spent his nights brooding over maps of the Valley of the Kings.

But as his enthusiasm grew, so did his commitment. Especially after World War I, when inflation ate away at his income and the sums spent on his work with Carter mounted higher and higher, he was tested. And though his test was only a financial one, still Carnarvon cared greatly about money, not to mention the fact that he had heavy expenses maintaining Highclere Castle, his ancestral estate.

In 1905, however, Carnarvon began with a simple proposition— that it would be very pleasant to sit in the shade, watching as objects of rare beauty were dug up from the earth. Using influence, he obtained permission to excavate in the hills near Hatshepsut's terraced temple. His plan was to go it alone with only a team of workers. But though he had no interest in engaging an archaeologist, or "learned man," as he called them, still and all as he traveled south to begin his dig, the paths of the earl and the outcast Carter had begun to converge.

PART FIVE

A USEFUL MAN

I am off to the races!

—THE FIFTH EARL OF CARNARVON,
IN A LETTER TO A FRIEND

The Fourth Earl of Carnarvon, 1831–1890.
Influential statesman and classical scholar.

———————

The Fifth Earl of Carnarvon, 1866–1923.
Patron of Howard Carter. Financed five years of digging in Thebes, followed by seven years of digging for King Tut's tomb.

———————

The Sixth Earl of Carnarvon, 1898–1987.
Lord Porchester until he succeeded to the title in 1923. International playboy who fell in love.

CHAPTER 10

A H, THE EARLS . . . IF THE SIXTH EARL OF CARNARVON HAD killed his father, the fifth earl, as he'd planned to, it's hard to say what would have become of Howard Carter.

The Fifth Earl of Carnarvon was one of many rich men interested in digging in Egypt. Carter had even worked for some of them during his early years—when he was still learning and developing—before he came into his own. But they were reasonable men engaged in reasonable endeavors. That is, they expected a reasonable return, in a reasonable amount of time, for a reasonable investment of cash.

The search for King Tut's tomb was not such an endeavor. It was begun amid warnings from every side that the Valley of the Kings was now exhausted: Even Gaston Maspero (who brought Carter and Carnarvon together) warned the earl that every royal tomb to be found there had been discovered.

There were good reasons for this pessimism, a pessimism that seemed to be confirmed by the results of the Carnarvon-Carter effort. To universal laughter, the spectacle of the futile excavation dragged on year after year for seven long years. The mounds of excavated rubble, meticulously sifted, piled higher and higher. Foot by foot, the area Carter had marked out was exposed to the bedrock.

The costs accumulated, the earl spent a fortune, and nothing was found. But still Carnarvon toasted Carter each season with the best champagne as he good-naturedly shrugged off the past failures. His slouch hat worn at a rakish angle, the sun glinting on his gold cigarette holder, Carnarvon would invariably irritate the gloomy Carter with his unbounded, amateurish enthusiasm. This would be their year, the earl was always sure; there was no telling what, in the coming season, they would uncover.

Who else would have been so foolish? The other men backing expeditions and buying antiquities in Egypt, the Pierpont Morgans and Theodore Davises, were too hardheaded to invest their money so unwisely.

But even say Carter had found someone willing to stake him in his impossible venture, who else would have put up with the moodiness of the embittered digger? For by the time Carnarvon and Carter teamed up, Carter had a reputation for being "difficult," to use the polite expression (many other, less polite adjectives were often applied to him).

By his own admission he had a "mauvaise [*sic*] caractère," which over the years had become worse owing to the strains of his life in Egypt, both physical and psychological. As he wrote apologetically in a letter to Percy Newberry, one of the few colleagues who remained a friend until the end: "Living alone as I do, is inducive to one letting the milk curdle." Which was putting it mildly: He was exacting, touchy, unjust, tyrannical, unkind—and brilliant. And what was worse, he knew it.

As Geanie Weigall (a famous beauty visiting her archaeologist brother, Arthur Weigall, in Egypt) wrote to a friend: "I do so dislike Carter. His manners are so aggressive and every word he utters is veiled with thin sarcasm." This in a social setting (Luxor's Winter Palace), and with a beautiful woman around whom men fluttered like moths. But on a dig—where Miss Weigall's charm did not exercise its restraining influence—Carter's "thin sarcasm" became rage at his colleagues' stupidity and ineptitude, real or imagined.

"I worked in the valley this AM. Carter took measurements for me until his extraordinary notions about projections caused such a violent disagreement between us that he refused to continue his assistance," a colleague (the draftsman Lindsley Hall) noted in his diary. "The man is unbearable," complained another (Henry Burton, one of the great archaeological photographers of all time). "But I must admit he showed me how to take a photograph I thought impossible."

In his dark moods, he could be terrifying. Even Carnarvon's daughter, Lady Evelyn, an admirer, said years after his death: "In the beginning I was in awe of him. Later, he made me rather afraid."

Carter was a diamond in the rough, a fact that the discerning earl appreciated. He understood his temperamental archaeologist and looked out for him as no one else would have during the lean years.

Who else but Carnarvon would have cut him into a sweet deal such as the treasure of the three princesses, for example? The cache, belonging to the Syrian wives of the warrior pharaoh Thutmosis III, was one of the most fabulous collections of ancient jewelry ever found.

Tomb robbers had scoured the desert after a flash flood, one of only three in the last thirty-five years. The streaming waters had dislodged many-ton boulders, tossing them aside as if they were pebbles. High up on the sides of the desert cliffs, a hiding place was exposed, where beautiful gold bracelets and earrings and necklaces had lain since the fifteenth century BC. After wrapping the treasure in dirty rags, the robbers carried it to an Egyptian dealer.

Normally, the collection (some 225 pieces) would have been

broken up and sold discreetly to different collectors over a number of years. But Carnarvon put up a huge amount of cash, enabling Carter secretly to buy the entire find from the Egyptian fence and sell it to New York's Metropolitan Museum of Art. Thus, thanks to Carnarvon, Carter received a hefty commission that took care of his financial worries. In addition, the deal established him as a major player on the antiquities scene until the end of his life.

But perhaps the most revealing moment in the relationship between the two men can be found at the time of the fifty-six-year-old Carnarvon's death. For who else—after being ordered out of Carter's house forever during a stormy quarrel—would have written a letter such as the one Carnarvon sent Carter:

> Friday Evening. [1923]
> I have been feeling very unhappy today and I did not know what to think or do, and then I saw Eve [Carnarvon's daughter] and she told me everything. I have no doubt that I have done many foolish things and I am very sorry. I suppose the fuss and worry [over the tomb's discovery] have affected me but there is only one thing I want to say to you which I hope you will always remember—whatever your feelings are or will be for me in the future my affection for you will never change.
> I'm a man with few friends and whatever happens nothing will ever alter my feeling for you. . . . I could not rest until I had written you.

Carnarvon's tact—he forgave Carter under the guise of asking for forgiveness; he was so careful not to wound his friend's dignity—would have been rare enough under ordinary circumstances. But when you consider that Carnarvon was a dying man at the time—he'd nicked a mosquito bite while shaving and had gotten septic poisoning—and consider his suffering when he wrote to

Carter, it makes his loyalty to the irascible, solitary archaeologist all the more extraordinary.

In his own way, George Edward Stanhope Molyneux Herbert, Fifth Earl of Carnarvon, was as unusual as Carter was in his. They were both one of a kind. Which made it all the more fortunate for Carter (and for Egyptology) that Carnarvon's son Lord Porchester did not act on the homicidal impulse he described sixty years later in his memoir, *No Regrets.*

For the most part, the memoir is ironic in tone, the incidents are all minor, the predominant quality is laughter and irreverence. Porchester describes his life, a life devoted to parties and practical jokes and love. But his childhood reminiscences are of interest in that, irony aside, we are able to see Carnarvon from the vantage point of his young son.

The grief of children! In their eyes, everything is raised to the tenth power. But in that exaggeration, there is sometimes more truth than in the view of less vulnerable adults.

As Porchester remembered, "Usually when I returned from school—accompanied by a very indifferent report—I would receive a summons to my father's study. He would be sitting at his desk and, as I came in, he would look up and say, 'My dear Porchester. As usual, your reports are very bad. Your writing is slovenly, your mathematics are appalling, and apparently you don't pay sufficient attention. I intend to make a useful man of you. Now you'd better take heed of this warning. I expect a distinct improvement, d'you understand? Off you go.' With that perfunctory statement, he would dismiss me back to the top floor where we children lived, ate, played and slept, using only the back staircase to make our escape to the outside world."

The boy's schoolwork didn't improve, however, and one day he saw the head gardener making birch rods. "I guessed what was about to happen and was desperately frightened when I entered the room. I was told to undress and my hands were tied down to the brass bedstead. Almost immediately my father came into the room and, ignoring me, went over to the birch rods, picking up each in turn and swishing it through the air until he seemed satisfied with the one he had selected.

"Standing back he performed a little on-the-spot jig, as if tautening his muscles, and then suddenly brought down the birch as hard as he could on to my bare bum. After the sixth stroke, he threw down the birch and went out of the room."

The tutor dressed the boy's wounds with ointment and tried to comfort him, but he remained obstinate. "This episode had a deep psychological effect upon me which was to last for many years. From that day onwards, I planned to kill my father and when a few weeks later I found him alone, I concealed myself in some bushes nearby in order to observe him, unseen. I had brought with me a little dagger which seemed well fitted to the task in hand. But I was fearful of two things. Firstly, being caught and then, should I succeed, being sent to Borstal [prison]. So I forsook the project."

We must remember that caning was common in England at the time, a standard practice, and that Carnarvon, despite some transcendent virtues, was very much a man of his time. The scene would have been typical down to Carnarvon's insistence that he would make his son "useful," a Victorian catchword usually coupled with "earnestness" in the categories of the day (an ideal that Oscar Wilde played with in the title of his wonderful farce *The Importance of Being Earnest*). The theory was that since the upper classes had been given so much, in return they had an obligation to accomplish something for the public good: noblesse oblige.

Poor Queen Victoria, however, had to face the fact that while this ideal was sometimes realized, just as often her nobility were pleasure-loving wastrels and bon vivants—including her own son Edward, who was always getting into scrapes. (To the end of her life, she reproached Edward for having killed his father. The typhoid was incidental, she claimed: Her beloved Albert had actually died from the shock of learning their nineteen-year-old son had lost his virginity—and with a French dancer to boot.)

Measured by Victorian standards, the life of the Fifth Earl of Carnarvon would have to be judged anything but "earnest" (at least the first half of it). At the time he was caning his idle son, he himself had achieved much that could have been written up in the society columns—His Lordship's yacht, His Lordship's horses, His Lordship's cars, and so forth. But he had done nothing that could match his own father's accomplishments. For Carnarvon's father, the fourth earl, cast a long shadow. He had been a brilliant classical scholar and a principled statesman who had served first as colonial secretary and then as Irish viceroy, becoming a close friend of Charles Stewart Parnell's and resigning when his liberal Irish policy was rejected by Parliament.

Perhaps in that cry of Carnarvon's, "I intend to make a useful man of you!" we can hear something of his exasperation with himself, for he had his father's enormous energy but not his intellect. He played no part in politics and "frankly detested the classics," according to his sister, Lady Burghclere. Their father, the fourth earl, she adds, was "too sensible to insist on his son pursuing indefinitely studies doomed to failure," so Carnarvon was left to follow his own interests. At Cambridge, his most notable achievement (besides the usual drinking bouts) was to find some beautiful wooden paneling in his rooms buried beneath layers of ugly wallpaper. The knowledge that would be important in his life was not scholarly or academic. If, as it has been observed, the Victorian gentleman would have been silent without the classics, then Carnarvon was mute.

Upon leaving school, he traveled widely. In Africa, he went in for the benighted sport of the upper classes then, big-game hunting (unsuccessfully: His life was saved at the last moment when he climbed a tree to escape a charging elephant). He crossed the Atlantic on his sailboat, the *Aphrodite*, and when he arrived in Argentina, he made plans to go around the Straits of Magellan. It was a suicidal project given the lightness of his craft and the waterway's rough seas, as an experienced sailor finally convinced him.

He gave it up and instead threw himself into the life of the capital, lingering in Buenos Aires before continuing his travels. It was a pattern we can see in these early years. He seemed to be trying to prove himself somehow, anyhow, taking up one pursuit after another, restlessly, without fixed purpose. . . . He became passionate about boxing matches, then opera, then aerial photography. There were passing affaires de cœur, which he took lightly, and successes at the racetrack, which he took seriously.

Whereas his father had "played" against the great statesmen of Europe, Carnarvon mingled with the betting underworld. As a friend (Sir Maurice Hankey) later said of him, "He was known to have pitted his brains against and outwitted the toughest bookies and 'crooks' on the turf." To which Hankey added mysteriously, "I do not know whether he is consistently cunning, or often ingenuous." Which is to say, he wasn't sure whether Carnarvon succeeded because he was shrewd or because he was a fool (with a fool's luck!).

Either way, fortune was on his side. He won the Ascot stakes, the Stewards' Cup at Goodwood, the Doncaster Cup, and the City and Suburban. He enjoyed the glory of leading his horses to the winner's circle. And he developed uncanny gambling instincts that would stand him in good stead—on the turf and off—along with a gambler's sangfroid, or cool.

"On one occasion in his youth," his sister related in her adoring eulogy, "he hired a boat to take him somewhere off the [Italian] coast to his ship lying far out to sea. He was alone, steering the little bark rowed by a couple of stalwart fishermen. Suddenly, when far removed from land, and equally distant from his goal, the two ruffians gave him the choice between payment of a large sum or being pitched into the water. He listened quietly, and motioned to them to pass his dressing-bag. They obeyed, already in imagination fingering the English 'Lord's' ransom.

"The situation was, however, reversed when he extracted, not a well-stuffed pocket-book, but a revolver, and pointing it at the pair sternly bade them row on, or he would shoot. The chuckle with which he recalled what was to him an eminently delectable episode, still remains with the hearer."

In the many disconnected episodes of Carnarvon's early life, we get the picture of a young man whose knowledge of the world is becoming broader and who was steadily becoming surer of himself. His travels brought him into contact with all sorts of people and made him a good judge of character. At first, all this accumulated experience seemed to be wasted. He put it to trivial ends—backing a dark horse or making a killing on the stock market. But in the long run, it all came into play in Egypt when he made the gamble of his life: a useful, earnest "bet" that even the fourth earl, statesman and classical scholar though he was, would have been hard put to match.

Not that Carnarvon originally had any such plan. After his death, high-sounding obituaries maintained that it was his love of history or archaeology that brought him to Egypt. But the truth is that two stubborn oxen brought him there.

Carnarvon was motoring in Germany at the time. The oxen, hitched to carts, stopped on a road across which a farmer was leading them. In his car—the third ever to be registered in England—Lord Carnarvon approached from the other side of a steep rise in the road. It was too late to stop when he saw them, so Carnarvon steered toward the edge of the road, trying to get around them. Some stones caught the wheels. Two tires burst, and the car turned over and fell on Carnarvon, while the servant accompanying him was thrown clear of the burning wreck.

As the unconscious earl lay half-crushed, his quick-thinking servant grabbed a pail of water from some passing workmen, dashed it over Carnarvon, whose clothes had caught fire, and then sent the workmen for help. Upon regaining consciousness—temporarily blinded, his legs burned, and his wrist broken—Carnarvon insisted first on knowing whether anyone else had been hurt (no one had); only after being informed of this did he allow himself to be taken to a town nearby.

So began a long period of invalidism. He developed problems with his chest and underwent many operations, which left him in a weakened state. His doctors recommended a warm, dry climate, and Egypt was a natural decision. "So much is Egypt the resort of the invalid," wrote the archaeologist Flinders Petrie, "that the guide-books seem all infected with invalidism; and to read their directions it might be supposed that no Englishman could walk a mile or more without an attendant of some kind."

Apart from the weather, Carnarvon chose Egypt because it was convenient, just across the Mediterranean, and had a large European community who welcomed the rich aristocrat. Cairo, with its opera house (built for the opening of the Suez Canal), its Gezira Sporting Club, its soirees and polo matches, offered Carnarvon all the distractions he was used to while he recovered his strength.

If the ruins entered into his decision at all, they were only another diversion Egypt had to offer. A visit to a "find" was more a social event than a scholarly one. "We had the whole Devonshire party to tea this afternoon to see the find," read a typical diary entry of the day. "The Duke and Duchess, her daughter Lady Gosford, and Lord Gosford and their daughter Lady Theodora Guest—with Mr. Weigall. . . . The duke, now a very old and broken man, is of course a great personage. The Duchess, so celebrated in her way, was a wonderful old woman—painted and enameled, with reddish wig, an old black hat, with painted lips—very keen to see everything."

Carnarvon fit in very well, along with his wife, Almina, who at that time was still in love with him. His feelings for her were more restrained, his attitude toward marriage being pragmatic. Or so it seemed from the fatherly advice he gave his son when the boy grew up and decided to marry for love. As Porchester recalled in his memoirs, his father took him aside and told him: "It seems to me totally unnecessary to go marrying an American, Porchester, and if what you tell me is correct, even more ridiculous to marry one with no money. If you are determined to do such a thing, I would have thought it much better to have picked a very rich one.... I can only tell you that before I consented to marry your mother, I got hold of Alfred de Rothschild and made some very stringent terms."

The incorrigible Porchester, though, followed his heart (and ended up living happily to an old age with his penniless sweetheart). Carnarvon's marriage, by contrast, was a mere matter of form by the time he met Carter. Almina was not at her husband's side when the great discovery took place; and she was "difficult to locate," as the gossip columnists would say, when he fell sick afterward. She finally arrived at his bedside at the last minute in a small Puss Moth airplane, an emergency mode of transportation.

But whatever emotional reversals took place in the Carnarvons' marriage, the financial benefits to the earl were lasting. For the Countess of Carnarvon, Almina, formerly Lady Wombwell, was actually the illegitimate daughter of a Rothschild, who could well afford Carnarvon's "stringent terms."

These included discharging his huge debts (150,000 pounds) and providing a dowry of 500,000 pounds (given its purchasing power at the time, an enormous sum), along with other financial settlements. On his death, Rothschild left Almina the bulk of his large fortune, including his London mansion and several country estates. Yet despite all this wealth, the prodigal Almina ended her days in poverty in a small apartment in Bristol—the court placed her in protective bankruptcy—forbidding any mention of Egypt to be made in her presence until the day of her death.

All of this was in the future, however. When in 1905 the well-heeled countess set out for Egypt in the company of her husband, she had no thought of her future poverty (or of her future lover, the tall, gaunt Tiger Denouston, charming, penniless, and also an invalid). And Carnarvon had no inkling that he would discover a royal tomb filled with art and treasure and the body of a boy-king lying in state for thirty-three hundred years.

One last glimpse of Carnarvon in his "pre-Egyptian" phase, though, reveals an important link connecting his past to his future. And again, this view of him was provided by his son. The boy, having accidentally knocked over the king at a children's party, was sent to a small attic room in disgrace.

The room was over the bedroom where Carnarvon's séances and palm readings and table rappings were held. If the strange voices and cries did nothing to soothe the boy, they shed an interesting light on his father. For Carnarvon was fascinated by the occult. He not only experimented with séances and levitation, but had his personal "supernormalist," Velma,* a well-known psychic who had given readings to such figures as the bandit president of Mexico, Pancho Villa, and the last czar of Russia. He would later claim that he had warned Carnarvon of his fate from the beginning. Which may or may not be true.

But Velma was only one of many to have issued such warnings. A member of London's Spiritual Alliance, Carnarvon often consulted psychics of many different descriptions. The famous medium and palmist Cheiro delivered messages to him from the Egyptian princess Meketaten (who died in childbirth in the fourteenth century BC). For effect, the medium could even produce the mummified hand that had scrawled them, though whether the severed limb was "the real thing" is anyone's guess. As is the whole

---

*All that is known of Velma's identity is that he was a psychic and a palmist. He himself often consulted Cheiro, Count Louis 1 Warner Hamon, 1866–1936, the most famous medium of the day.

question of communications from the other side, Egyptian magic, curses, and "supernormalism," as it was called at the time.

The one prediction that was beyond dispute, however—a matter of public record—was the one about Carnarvon made not by a psychic or medium but by Carter's colleague and enemy Arthur Weigall. Carter hated him, perhaps, more than all his other enemies put together. He was everything Carter was not, eloquent, sure of himself in society, handsome—a ladies' man and a romantic, who married first a beautiful American woman wandering throughout Europe (with whom he had five children) and then a brash composer of popular musical songs.

In 1923, Weigall, watching Carnarvon laughing and joking at Tut's tomb, dreamily predicted that the earl had six weeks to live. His words were recalled—and created a sensation—when, almost six weeks to the day, Carnarvon died in agony and delirium.

Weigall had uttered his prophecy without thinking; he could give no explanation for its accuracy. But if he had premeditated some sort of plan to revenge himself on Carter, he could not have come up with a better one. Nothing upset Carter more than such speculation, which he would always indignantly dismiss as "tommyrot!" For unlike his patron, Carter was not a "believer" in the supernatural—at least not in a literal, simple sense.

Egypt always held mystery for Carter, but that mystery derived from understandable causes—the country's beauty, the stark deserts and ancient ruins, the awe that came over him in the tombs and temples.

Nowhere else was one as aware that "we stand between the eternity of the past and the eternity of the future," as Amelia Edwards, founder of the Egyptian Exploration Fund, put it. Living for long periods of time on such intimate terms with the past—as Carter was to and as Ms. Edwards had before him—magnified this feeling many times over.

An excavator's state of mind was necessarily altered, call it psychological, call it mystical. As Weigall described it, descending into an Egyptian tomb that had been sealed for thousands of years was like walking through a tear in the curtain of time: The dried flowers strewn over the broken coffins, the leavings of the last funeral meal, and the bodies ravaged by ancient robbers all produced an impression that was uncanny and oppressive. In fact, more than one excavator who had had the experience—Jones, Ayrton, Weigall, Carter, for example—stated that at first he was overcome with the feeling of being an intruder, of committing sacrilege. This, together with an almost physical impulse to get out, to rush back through the winding passages and into the light of day.

CHAPTER 11

B UT EVEN ABOVEGROUND, IN EGYPT THE LIGHT OF DAY WAS darkened with memories. During the time of the pharaohs, its barren wastes had been the setting for meditation, prayer, and magic. First came pharaoh's sorcerers and the temple recluses. For three thousand years they roamed the desert, seeking visions from the oracles of Hathor, Amun, and Ptah.

Then came the Christians: monks living in the ruins of pagan shrines (Christian monasticism began here); hermits practicing fantastic forms of self-denial; and stylites—half-mad holy men living exposed for decades on the tops of pillars, their food hoisted up by means of palm-frond ropes.

The Muslims followed, with mystical Sufi orders and mosques rising in the midst of pharaonic temples—in fact, built from the ancient stones. And finally the archaeologists arrived, lowered into their tombs by means of these same palm-fiber ropes, as Ms. Edwards recounted in her memoir. Writing the year Carter came to Egypt, she described this daily encounter with another reality. At every step in Egypt, the excavator is aware of the bejeweled and mummified dead "just below the surface, waiting to be discovered. Whether you go up the great river [the Nile], or strike off to east or west across the desert, your horizon is always bounded by mounds, or by ruins, or by ranges of mountains honey combed with tombs.

"If you but stamp your foot upon the sands, you know that it probably awakens an echo in some dark vault or corridor untrodden for three or four thousand years. The exploration is a kind of chase. You think you have discovered a scent. You follow it. You lose and you find it again. You go through every phase of suspense, excitement, hope, disappointment, exultation.

"With the keenness of a North American Indian, [you must use your] wits, your eyes. You sight a depression in the soil, splinters of limestone, perhaps the wreck of a tomb? Baskets are loaded at the bottom of a tomb and hauled up, spilling half their contents on the way up. . . . [The workers,] the children and their parents go home but you remain in the dark hole, with nothing to eat since seven o clock in the morning and a furious headache. . . .

"The next morning [it is the same] again and again, one, two, three weeks . . . [in Carter's case, for years]. You descend into tomb pits, one hundred or one hundred and fifty feet deep, crawl through subterraneous passages. . . . There is a rope you must trust to: a flimsy twist of palm fibre which becomes visibly thinner from the strain and goes further down as if into a mine . . . and you find Nobles from the time of Thutmoses II? [1500 BC] Ramses II? [1260 BC] lying in three coffins . . . alabaster vases, libation vessels—or only a broken coffin, a handful of bones with the jewels, amulets, papyri gone! There is an inscription on one of the walls of the passages. . . . Perhaps a new [hitherto unknown] chapter of The Book of The Dead. . . . Or a genealogical table. A link in the royal family of a dynasty, or [the records of] a Greek or Roman tourist. . . ."

There was no telling what would be found next. This sense of anything being possible, of continual suspense, was shared by Carter. He experienced it almost from the beginning, and nowhere more strongly than in the Valley of the Kings. Over the course of decades, he developed a special feeling for the Valley. For him, it had a nature, a personality, all its own: It was capricious, disappointing the most strenuous efforts and then suddenly revealing some long hidden secret when one was at the point of giving up. The Valley had, Carter would say privately, a "mystical potency": an uncanny power to which he became attuned over many years of digging. He worked at many sites, but no other place had the same draw.

What saved him was his strong grip on reality: His love for the Valley had no admixture of superstitious dread. Weigall, by contrast, gave complete rein to his imagination. At the end of 1911, Weigall's breakdown began on a train returning to the Valley, where he had been living for many years. He turned around and fled to Cairo, unable to face yet another encounter with the stark cliffs sheltering the ancient royal tombs. Soon afterward, he left Egypt on sick leave.

Weigall was not alone—this susceptibility was an occupational hazard. Georges Legrain, for example, the service archaeologist who spent some twenty years working at the Karnak temple, also gave way. About the time that he discovered the "Karnak cache"— some six thousand huge statues hidden under the temple ground—rumors began to circulate about his erratic behavior. Scandalized, Maspero rebuked him for participating in ancient rituals. "Legrain is a fool—I will wash his head!" Maspero fumed in a letter to a colleague. "He has gone out of his mind!"

Apparently, Legrain had practiced his indiscretions in a side chapel of Karnak, the three-thousand-year-old temple to the lion-headed goddess Sekhmet. It was a small structure with a tiny opening in the granite ceiling shedding a dim light on the goddess with her enigmatic smile. Cracks could be seen near her shoulders where her statue was restored. Two basket boys had died during its excavation (buried by a sudden cave-in), and their father, blaming Sekhmet, vented his rage on her image.

Chanting before the goddess, Legrain had recited the ancient spells as if he were a priest of the goddess, while two visiting Frenchwomen kissed her feet.

In a letter dated March 1911, Maspero wrote to Legrain: "Everyone—natives and foreigners—ridicules both you who indulge yourself daily in these eccentricities and the Department that allows you to do so."

But mad or sane, Legrain managed to stay at his post and perform valuable restoration work. The young Oxford-trained archaeologist Edward Ayrton was not as fortunate. Joseph Lindon Smith, a painter of archaeological scenes, remembered that "Ayrton was not popular at night. By consensus, his cot was placed a long distance away from the rest of us. He had dreadful nightmares in which he shrieked in fluent Chinese." The Chinese was incidental (Ayrton was brought up in the East by a diplomat father), but the nightmares were perhaps a sign of what was to come. Eventually Ayrton quit Egypt, his nerves overstrained and his personality warped. In a letter to a friend, Smith related that at the opening of Pharaoh Horemheb's tomb, "Ayrton had suddenly gone mad. . . . We think he has gone off his head really."

Following this, Ayrton left Egypt, unable to bear the solitude of the sites, worn out by the intense pressure of his patron, Theodore Davis, to find royal tombs, and unable to descend any longer into the underground passages. Ayrton died soon afterward in Ceylon during a hunting expedition—the circumstances of the young man's death being, it goes without saying, suspicious to some, perfectly normal to others.

In an essay entitled "The Malevolence of Ancient Spirits," Arthur Weigall cataloged a long list of strange incidents—of mummies being removed from houses where desperately sick children then recover, of mummified animals bursting as their live counterparts suddenly appeared nearby, and so on—incidents that the skeptical may dismiss as coincidence or hearsay.

One story, however, was especially noteworthy in that it needs no supernatural sanction. With or without sorcery, it reveals the way the daily work of the diggers had the potential to induce a kind of madness: "We were engaged in clearing out a vertical tomb-shaft," Weigall recalled, "which had been cut through the rock underlying the sandy surface of the desert. . . . At sunset I gave the order to stop work for the night, and I was about to set out on my walk back to the camp when the foreman came to tell me that a mummied hand had been laid bare, and it was evident that we were about to come upon an interred body.

"By lamplight, therefore, the work was continued; and presently we had uncovered the sand-dried body of an old woman, who by her posture appeared to have met with a violent death. It was evident that this did not represent the original burial in the tomb, the bottom of the shaft not yet having been reached; and I conjectured that the corpse before us had been thrown from above at some more recent date—perhaps in Roman times [that is, 30 BC–AD 342, considered recent by Egyptian standards]—when the shaft was but half full of debris, and in course of time had become buried by blown sand and natural falls of rock.

"The workmen were now waiting for their evening meal, but I was anxious to examine the body and its surroundings carefully. I therefore sent all but one of the men back to the camp, and descended into the shaft by means of a rope ladder, carrying with me a hurricane lamp to light my search. In the flickering rays of the lamp . . . the old woman lay upon her back, her arms outstretched upwards, as though they had stiffened thus in some convulsion, the fingers being locked together. Her legs were thrust outwards rigidly, and the toes were cramped and bent. The features of the face were well preserved, as was the whole body; and long black hair descended to her bony shoulders in a tangled mass. Her mouth was wide open, the two rows of teeth gleaming savagely in the uncertain light, and the hollow eye-sockets seemed to stare upwards, as though fixed upon some object of horror. . . . [Despite the passage of thousands of years, the faces of mummies are often extraordinarily expressive. One has only to compare the peaceful, dignified expression on the face of Seti I with the agonized features of Pharaoh Se'qe'enre, who died of horrible wounds in battle.]

"Just as I was completing my search I felt a few drops of rain fall, and at the same time realised that the wind was howling and whistling above me. A rain storm in Upper Egypt is a very rare occurrence, and generally it is of a torrential character. If I left the body at the bottom of the shaft, I thought to myself, it would be soaked and destroyed; and since, as a specimen, it was well worth preserving, I decided to carry it to the surface, where there was a hut in which it could be sheltered. . . . I called out to the man whom I had told to wait for me on the surface, but received no reply. Either he had misunderstood me and gone home, or else the noise of the wind prevented my voice from reaching him. Large spots of rain were now falling, and there was no time for hesitation. I therefore lifted the body on to my back, the two outstretched arms passing over my shoulders and the linked fingers clutching, as it were, at my chest. I then began to climb up the rope ladder, and as I did so I noticed with something of a qualm that the old woman's face was peeping at me over my right shoulder and her teeth seemed about to bite my right ear.

"I had climbed about half the distance when my foot dislodged a fragment of rock from the side of the shaft, and, as luck would have it, the stone fell right upon the lamp, smashing the glass and putting the light out. The darkness in which I found myself was intense, and now the wind began to buffet me and to hurl the sand into my face. With my right hand I felt for the woman's head and shoulder, in order to hitch the body more firmly on to my back, but to my surprise my hand found nothing there. At the same moment I became conscious that the hideous face was grinning at me over my left shoulder, my movements, I suppose, having shifted it; and without further delay, I blundered and scrambled to the top of the shaft in a kind of panic.

"No sooner had I reached the surface than I attempted to relieve myself of my burden. The wind was now screaming past me and the rain was falling fast. I put my left hand up to catch hold of the corpse's shoulder, and to my dismay found that the head had slipped round once more to my right, and the face was peeping at me from that side. I tried to remove the arms from around my neck, but, with ever increasing horror, I found that the fingers had caught in my coat and seemed to be holding on to me. A few moments of struggle ensued, and at last the fingers released their grip. Thereupon the body swung round so that we stood face to face, the withered arms still around my neck and the teeth grinning at me through the darkness. A moment later I was free, and the body fell back from me, hovered a moment, as it were, in mid air, and suddenly disappeared from sight. It was then that I realised that we had been struggling at the very edge of the shaft, down which the old woman had now fallen, and near which some will say that she had been wildly detaining me."

To this suggestion—that the murdered old woman was trying to drag Weigall into the pit into which she had been thrown so long before—Carter would have snorted his usual line: "Tommyrot!" Though he himself was a man of much imagination, it was just this kind of speculation he hated. And it was just this kind of speculation that would dog his footsteps from the moment he made his great discovery.

Again and again, he would be forced to refute occult theories about Tut's tomb. He fought "the good fight," citing authorities that ranged from chemists and scientists (who confirmed that the tomb contained no ancient poisons, powders, or deadly metals) to the pope (who declared that the excavation of Tut was not a blasphemous exhumation, but a resurrection).

If there was a single statement that sums up Carter's position, it was the one he made at the end of his career: "Imagination is a good servant, but it is a bad master." Weigall fell under its spell and had a nervous breakdown. But Carter was conscious that it was he himself who summoned up whatever spirits inhabited the tombs. For him, they were part of the dreamlike interplay of light and shadow that made Egypt eternally intriguing.

This attitude was in evidence from the very beginning. Carter was sensitive to his surroundings; they worked on him, but he was never overwhelmed. In his abandoned autobiographical sketch, he described how he felt when he arrived at his first assignment: "The warm, dry and motionless atmosphere [of the tomb where he slept] made me conscious of a strange sensation as I lay somewhat bewildered in my new surroundings, endeavouring to sleep upon a roughly made palm-branch bedstead. That first night I watched from my bed the brilliant starry heavens visible through the doorway. I listened to the faint flutterings of the bats that flitted around our rock-chamber and, in imagination I called up strange spirits from the ancient dead until the first gleam of dawn when, from sheer fatigue I fell asleep."

There were not many sleepless nights after that. Very simply, he worked too hard to sit up listening to the bats—or to summon strange spirits. He was exhausted by the end of a day that was filled with difficult, practical tasks. Perhaps this was the element in his character that grounded him—his practical orientation. In reading the scores of inspection and excavation reports he filed over the years, one is struck by two facts: first, how good he was at what he did; and second, how often his work required purely technical skills.

To pick an example almost at random, take his *Report of Work Done in Upper Egypt, 1902–1903, Edfu Temple* (the most complete example of an ancient temple standing since antiquity). The report is typical in its precision, its specificity—and its misspelling: "Many of the roof slabs in this temple have long been cracked, their excessive span having in the long course of centuries proved two [*sic*] great a strain on the sandstone of which they are made.

"May 1901. Temple strutted with timber until the necessary girders and stirrups could be obtained each stone slab pierced by a 0m.05 cent. boring machine. Iron stirrups passed through, though bolted below by a nut and plate and fixed above to iron girders etc.

"159 L.E. [Egyptian pounds] prices for girders, stirrups, timed and year wages to workmen freight and transport . . . etc."

He may confuse the spelling of "two" and "too" (his letters and reports are filled with misspelled English words—next to Latin and French phrases, affectations picked up from his gentlemen colleagues). But he made no mistakes when it came to the technical side of his work. Or, for that matter, its artistic one. His drawings, watercolors, and paintings far surpass his colleagues' work not only for accuracy, but in their feeling for ancient Egyptian line and color.

His portraits of the ancient royal Thutmoside family brought them to life. His studies of the temples and tombs were evocative and panoramic. And the details he captured were amazing: Beneath the weight of a crouching cat, we see the papyrus plant bend in the ancient swamps, birds fluttering overhead. A vulture carved in a temple wall, its wings outstretched, hovers over a modern bird perched in a crevice of the ruined wall. Row upon row of ancient workmen are recorded down to the last man, forty-two in a gang, with the foreman, arms outstretched, standing high above them.

He was not a great artist; connoisseurs (such as Thomas Hoving, director of the Metropolitan Museum of Art in the 1970s) may find fault with this or that aspect of his work. But for what it was meant to be, a record of the ancient ruins, it was wonderful.

It can be imagined, then, how such a man as Carter, someone possessed of artistic temperament as well as practical intelligence, could be driven to exasperation by a sensation-seeking public.

From the moment of Carnarvon's death, he was barraged with questions from reporters dwelling on curses and ancient poisons and doom.

Tut's mummy was found to have a scar from a healed lesion. As the medical report from the first autopsy reads: "On the left cheek, just in front of the earlobe, is a round depression which has slightly raised edges, the skin is discoloured. It is not possible to say what the nature of this lesion may have been. . . ." Carnarvon was fatally bitten on his cheek as well—but on which one? By the time Dr. Derry performed the autopsy on Tut, no one could say for sure. Half a year earlier, Carnarvon had been buried in the hills overlooking Highclere (as a *Daily Express* reporter flew overhead, taking pictures of his widow, Almina—for once without her lover, Tiger—as she knelt beside the grave).

Undeterred, the tragic chorus crying, "The curse!" pointed to other "phenomena," from the inexplicable to the ludicrous: Cairo's lights suddenly went out as Lord Carnarvon died. They were always going out, it may be objected! Yes, but consider this, comes the believer's imperturbable reply: All four Cairo districts were affected at once, an unusual occurrence. Moreover, one to which Lord Cromer drew attention by announcing that the engineer on duty could offer no explanation.

A Paris couturier (Léon Bakst) planned a showing of his "Isis collection" (designs à la Tut) and died the night before its opening.

Carnarvon's private secretary, Sir Richard Bethel, aged forty-six, was found dead at his club. It was a punishment, proclaimed the famous psychic Cheiro, for his having taken objects from the tomb.

But even saying we accept the supernatural viewpoint, there is still another way of looking at events. For according to Egyptian beliefs, to be forgotten, to die and be consigned to oblivion, was a terrible fate. Ramesses II, perhaps the most megalomaniacal of the pharaohs, built monuments from one end of Egypt to the other.

Determined that his name should live forever, he covered them with cartouches carved so deeply in the stone that no one could usurp them. And even humbler Egyptians put great emphasis on being remembered, on their names echoing until the end of time.

Unlike the impious Greeks, who would sometimes mirthfully record that the deceased was a boozer and a mad dog, lustful beyond belief, someone who never said no to a wager, and so on, the Egyptians were concerned for the fate of their souls. Wandering among their graves, one is continually beseeched by the long dead to utter their names or to pour out some water or wine for them before the gods.

Before the discovery of his tomb, Tutankhamun was one of the least known of the pharaohs, his name familiar to perhaps half a dozen scholars. Afterward, he eclipsed even Ramesses in fame. Looked at in this way, Carter could truthfully claim that he deserved a blessing, not a curse, for having brought about the boy-king's resurrection.

But if Carter was too practical to greatly concern himself with such speculation, he was also practical enough to humor the superstitious Carnarvon during their years of working together. During a return visit to England, Carter was a guest at Highclere, where he shot, rode—and attended séances in the East Anglia bedroom. Carnarvon's son, the naughty Porchester, now a grown-up and a soldier on duty in Mesopotamia, was home on leave.

This time Porchester did not listen from the attic; he was invited to attend. As he remembered: "I watched [Lady] Helen Cunliffe-Owen put into a trance on an occasion when Howard Carter was also present. It had been an eerie, not to say unpleasant, experience which had shaken me considerably. One moment she had been her normal self, the next her features had become strained and white. Suddenly she had started talking in an unknown tongue which, to everyone's astonishment, Howard Carter had pronounced as being Coptic."

Carter would probably not have been able to distinguish Coptic, the last form of ancient Egyptian, from Celtic. He knew a little about the written form of ancient Egyptian, the hieroglyphs—but only what was useful in his excavations (when it came to any question about inscriptions, he turned to such experts as James Breasted or Sir Alan M. Gardiner, who were both working in Egypt during this time).

The pronunciation of the hieroglyphs (which ceased to be written in the fourth century AD) was and remains a disputed matter, the language having been written without vowels. Though as a spoken language, Coptic lingered on until the eleventh century AD, that still leaves us with the question of where Carter would have heard its sounds.

The only possible answer would be in church, where Coptic is still sometimes used in the Egyptian orthodox liturgy: an unlikely answer, since Carter's religion was digging. Letters, journals, diaries, and reports show him at the sites (even at Christmas), not listening to the chanting of monks.

A more likely explanation is that he was too polite—or too politic—to disappoint his patron. It is revealing to consider this question in the light of another incident, also from his early years, the years when he was still struggling to forge a career: the visit of Emma Andrews to Amenhotep II's tomb, which Carter was restoring. Ms. Andrews asked Carter about some hieroglyphs covering a coffin, and Carter, perhaps not wanting to disappoint her, perhaps wanting to be seen in a more authoritative light, "translated" the inscription as an ancient Egyptian curse. However, there was no such curse on the coffin lid!

The fact of the matter is that Carter was not above lying when it suited his purpose. It is a side of his character that we will encounter with a shock of surprise later on, when much more is at stake.

Even with the whole world watching—after the discovery of

Tut's tomb—he could be deceitful. He could secretly enter the inner burial chamber and then replace the blocking for the official opening. He could not only pocket "small" objects from the tomb (his niece would secretly return them after his death), but also attempt to steal one of its great masterpieces: the wooden portrait bust of the young king emerging from a lotus.

Such actions should not serve to indict him. They only remind us of his complexity as a human being. They are a caveat—do not take the man at face value. He was like one of the desert cliffs or Delta mounds he excavated. More was going on beneath the surface than you saw.

He wrote in his autobiographical sketch that sometimes he became discouraged at the hardships of his life as an excavator; sometimes he questioned his own wisdom in choosing a profession other than that of his father. It was more than a new profession he was trying to achieve, though, it was a new identity. He was trying to reinvent himself but felt ill equipped for the part he wanted to play in life. He knew his manners were gauche and his education poor, but still he would not give up. A gentleman colleague wrote in a letter: "He [Carter] doesn't hesitate to pick his last hollow tooth with a match stalk during dinner, bite bread that is so hard you can hardly cut it with a chopper, and help himself to whisky in an absent minded fashion, emptying half the bottle into his tumbler, then laugh and say he wasn't thinking and pour it back again into the bottle, spilling a lot."

"I have never accepted Carter as a colleague," wrote another, the respected archaeologist George Andrew Reisner, at the time digging in Egypt for Harvard University and the Boston Museum.

Carter knew there were those who disliked and scorned him, but from the beginning he was determined to beat them at their own game. After the discovery, when he became a public figure, there were unkind comments about his "plummy" accent (Americans would say "fruity"): It was Carter's version of an upper-class accent, of course, which he affected along with the silk breast pocket handkerchiefs and the cigarette holders and even the body language that he copied from Carnarvon. In terms of Carter's new identity, Carnarvon's aristocratic style was just as important to the excavator as what he learned on the ancient mounds. For the earl served not only as Carter's patron, but as a role model, a way of presenting himself to the world.

If Carnarvon could be irritating to Carter, sitting down in the desert to dine aristocratically on bacon, tongue, curried fowl, wine, biscuits, and Oriental pickles—courtesy of Fortnum & Mason—and in the middle of the day to boot; if Carnarvon's enthusiasm in the face of dismal failures could likewise get on Carter's nerves—if the earl's séances and table rappings had to be borne—Carter could not have achieved what he did without him.

The genial earl came to Egypt for his health; the gloomy excavator was there to find his livelihood—purposes that grew in scope and depth by the time their paths crossed. It was a meeting that, in retrospect, seemed fated. It was as if they had been summoned by the boy-king, who, underground, waited for them in all his unresurrected splendor—a mystical notion that would have pleased Carnarvon no end but that would have made poor Carter suffer.

PART SIX

A FINAL THROW OF THE DICE

How did they meet?
How does anyone meet?
—FROM DENIS DIDEROT'S *Jacques the Fatalist*

CHAPTER 12

1905
Southern Egypt

T WO MEN WHO DID NOT KNOW EACH OTHER PROVIDED ENTER-
tainment for the gossips of Luxor during the 1905 digging
season. One was the dour ex-inspector Carter, hawking his
watercolors and taking "superior" tourists around the sights.
Though it was in his interest to be polite, many times an unconsidered remark would bring on an outburst of Carter's temper, sending the "superior" tourist or potential buyer running for cover and
leaving the ex-inspector without his fee, perhaps, but with the satisfaction of having spoken his mind.

The second figure of fun for the locals was the silly, rich British
earl who could be seen raising clouds of dust in the desert hills
near Deir el-Bahri.

Although Carnarvon had hired a large band of workers and basket boys, anyone could tell that he was an amateur. Digging first in
one spot and then suddenly switching to another, he proceeded er-
ratically, without any method to his madness.

Or so it seemed. A casual observer of this new farce in the
desert had no way of knowing that though no archaeologist directed Carnarvon's excavation, the earl was getting advice from a
more reliable source—the ancient priests themselves, who whis-
pered their messages to him through his psychics and supernor-
malists. The result was that after Carnarvon's first season was over

and the dust had settled, what he had to show for his work was . . . well, a mummified cat.

An unimpressive find, perhaps—weighed on the scales of the uninitiated. But if we consider the account of Arthur Weigall, the new inspector, then Carnarvon's first discovery might be seen as a portent of things to come, a find in keeping with the earl's mystical propensities and psychic energy.

"Lord Carnarvon . . . discovered a hollow wooden figure of a large black cat, which we recognized . . . to be the shell in which a real embalmed cat was confined.

"The figure looked more like a small tiger as it sat in the sunlight at the edge of the pit in which it had been discovered, glaring at us with its yellow painted eyes. Its body was covered all over with a thick coating of smooth, shining pitch, and we could not at first detect the line along which the shell had been closed after it had received the mortal remains of the sacred animal within; but we knew from experience that the joint passed completely round the figure—from the nose, over the top of the head, down the back, and along the breast—so that, when opened, the two sides would fall apart in equal halves.

"The somber figure was carried down to the Nile and across the river to my house, where by a mistake on the part of my Egyptian servant, it was deposited in my bedroom. Returning home at the dead of night, I here found it seated in the middle of the floor directly in my path from the door to the matches; and for some moments I was constrained to sit beside it, rubbing my shins and my head.

"I rang the bell but receiving no answer, I walked to the kitchen, where I found the servants grouped distractedly around the butler, who had been stung by a scorpion and was in the throes of that short but intense agony. Soon he passed into a state of delirium and believed himself to be pursued by a large grey cat, a fancy which did not surprise me since he had so lately assisted in carrying the figure to its ill-chosen resting-place in my bedroom.

"At length, I retired to bed, but the moonlight which now entered the room through the open French windows fell full upon the black figure of the cat; and for some time I lay awake watching the peculiarly weird creature as it stared past me at the wall. I estimated its age to be considerably more than three thousand years, and I tried to picture to myself the strange people who, in those distant times, had fashioned this curious coffin for a cat which had been to them half pet and half household god. . . .

"In the distance I could hear the melancholy wails of the unfortunate butler imploring those around him to keep the cat away from him, and it seemed to me that there came a glitter into the eyes of the figure as the low cries echoed down the passage.

"At last I fell asleep, and for about an hour all was still. Then, suddenly, a report like that of a pistol rang through the room. I started up, and as I did so a large grey cat sprang either from or on to the bed, leapt across my knees, dug its claws into my hands, and dashed through the window into the garden. At the same moment I saw by the light of the moon that the two sides of the wooden figure had fallen apart and were rocking themselves to a standstill upon the floor, like two great empty shells. Between them sat the mummified figure of a cat, the bandages which swathed it round being ripped open at the neck, as though they had been burst outward.

"I sprang out of bed and rapidly examined the divided shell; and it seemed to me that the humidity in the air here on the bank of the Nile had expanded the wood which had rested in the dry desert so long, and had caused the two halves to burst apart with the loud noise which I had heard. Then, going to the window, I scanned the moonlit garden; and there in the middle of the pathway I saw, not the grey cat which had scratched me, but my own pet tabby, standing with arched back and bristling fur, glaring into the bushes, as though she saw ten feline devils therein.

"I will leave the reader to decide whether the great cat was the malevolent spirit which ... had burst its way through the bandages and woodwork and had fled into the darkness; or whether the torn embalming cloths represented the natural destructive work of Time, and the grey cat was a night wanderer which had strayed into my room and had been frightened by the easily explained bursting apart of the two sides of the ancient Egyptian figure."

Naturally or supernaturally, the cat was out of the coffin; and with the necropolis feline as tutelary spirit, Carnarvon's new career was under way. He continued digging with undiminished enthusiasm—though he uncovered nothing of importance (or rather nothing that he considered important). Among his finds, though, there was an old wooden tablet that had cracked in half—but what of it? Carnarvon was looking for some beautiful objet d'art and tossed the tablet into a basket along with the other ancient debris, potsherds, and scraps of mummy bandages.

His carelessness caused three crucial lines to be lost, for the tablet is inscribed. On one side were the sayings of the sage Ptah-hotep, while the other contained a record from one of the least documented periods in Egyptian history—the national rebellion against the invading Hyksos, nomadic "shepherd kings" who ruled Egypt for some two and a half centuries (ca. 1800 BC). It will become known as "the Carnarvon Tablet," though at the time it was only the Carnarvon washboard, some ancient junk he dropped off at the inspector's office on his way back to Cairo. As it turned out, though, Carnarvon's washboard would be his calling card with Carter.

Weigall, as inspector responsible for overseeing the Valley of the Kings, wrote indignantly to the linguist Francis Llewellyn Griffith, "Towards the end of the work [Carnarvon's dig], I had to go away, and when I returned to Luxor, Lord Carnarvon had gone, leaving his antiquities in my office. There was a basket full of odds and ends. Amongst these, stuffed anyhow into the mouth of the basket was this tablet, in two pieces, and I am sure this rough handling is responsible for some of the flaking. A sadder instance of the sin of allowing amateurs to dig could not be found. Lord Carnarvon does his best, and sits over his work conscientiously; but that is not enough."

Griffith replied, "It is grievous to think the plaque may have been perfect when found. I have worked at it again since I wrote to you . . . the three lines from the middle are a great loss. It is the most important document we have next to the el Kab Ahmosi inscriptions."

Sir Alan M. Gardiner, the most respected linguistic authority of the day, wrote in the *Journal of Egyptian Archaeology,* "No single inscription has been more important in the last ten years."

The grieved linguists pored over the now only half-comprehensible boasts of the warrior Kamose (a distant ancestor of Tutankhamun's), who "at the time of the perfuming of the mouth [early morning] pounced on the foreign enemy like a hawk, destroying his wall, slaying his people, carrying off slaves, cattle, fat and honey—the hearts of my soldiers rejoicing." Meanwhile, Carnarvon—oblivious to the archaeological suffering he had caused, enthusiastically made boasts of his own. Speculating on the endless possibilities before him, he announced, "I would rather discover a royal tomb than win the Derby!"

The archaeologists appealed to Maspero, who, continually harassed for funds, was not anxious to alienate Carnarvon. On the one hand, a wealthy patron was not easy to come by. On the other, Maspero was a scholar sensitive to his colleagues' concerns. What was more, he saw the situation as a way of rehabilitating Carter, whose talents he valued and whose situation he deplored. Why not arrange it so that Carnarvon's excavations were carried out by Carter—surely a satisfactory arrangement from every point of view, Maspero decided.

Carnarvon agreed immediately—a "learned man" was just what he required since he hadn't had the time to sufficiently "get up" on the subject. Though he'd heard the gossip about Carter, the man's stubbornness attracted him rather than otherwise—for he was unconventional himself, down to the rebellious brown shoes he wore to Ascot.

For Carter, who had been languishing in the twilight world of dealers and picturesque watercolors since his resignation as inspector in 1905, this opportunity was nothing less than a resurrection. He went to meet Carnarvon at Luxor's Winter Palace, where they sat on the hotel's Nile-side terrace and discussed the upcoming 1909 season. And where they took stock of each other. Though "Dr. Johnny"—Carnarvon's personal physician, whom he frequently kept by his side—hovered in the background, Carter could see that the nobleman was determined and energetic, if inexperienced. And Carnarvon immediately liked Carter, who obviously lived with only one thought in mind—to make a great find.

The American entrepreneur Theodore Davis had held the excavation concession for the Valley itself since 1902 and showed no sign of relinquishing it. For the time being, they would have to dig around the Valley proper: in the cliffs above Hatshepsut's temple, at the bottom of the slopes of Dra Abu el-Naga, the Birabi, the Assasif, and at the edge of the cultivation, the lush green land flooded by the Nile. It was not the Valley of the Kings proper, but still there was no telling what they might find here. Carter unrolled his map, while Carnarvon—defying both Dr. Johnny and the odds—raised a glass to their partnership.

And so the match was made, courtesy of Maspero, archaeological cupid, with good results soon following. "After perhaps ten days work we came upon what proved to be an untouched tomb," the thrilled Carnarvon wrote of "his first." "I shall never forget the sight. There was something extraordinarily modern about it. Several coffins were in the tomb, but the first that arrested our attention was a white brilliantly painted coffin with a pall loosely thrown over it, a bouquet of flowers lying just at its foot. There these coffins had remained untouched and forgotten for two thousand five hundred years."

Over the next seven years, from 1907 until the outbreak of World War I, they made many such discoveries in the Theban hills. Carnarvon in his elegant Edwardian getup hovered nearby, while Carter like a conjuror brought up from the earth mummies, mirrors, game boards, statues, jewelry, musical instruments, and magical oars—along with the so-called beds of Osiris, the resurrected god of the dead torn to bits by his evil brother, Seth, and pieced together by his wife-sister, Isis. The hollow wooden Osiride boxes (shaped in the god's form) were filled with seeded soil that began to sprout millennia ago under their mummy bandages, a symbol of the irrepressible, enduring nature of life and its triumph—even in the tomb—over death.

There was almost no knowing what or who would appear next as the dour archaeologist presented his patron with the artifacts of a vanished world. Carnarvon watched, awed, deferential; Carter was gruff, focused, sometimes aloof, sometimes taking the time to explain. This was the nature of their relationship from now until the end. A colleague (Arthur Mace) recorded later that when he was working with the two in Tut's tomb, Carnarvon was always wandering about, pestering Carter with questions, and that Carter "spoke to him as if he were a naughty child!"

By that time, they had lived through more than sixteen years of shared disappointments, victories, and anxieties: Would a fragile antiquity survive as sand was brushed from its surface? Would the overhanging tomb masonry collapse or hold? Which museums should receive one of the sixty-four painted coffins from tomb

#37? How best to pack up the Amunemheb statue—a breathtaking bronze of a naked young boy, his shaven head thrown back, his lithe body striding forward, his expression alert, intent, alive.

But through all the years of Carter's preliminary work with Carnarvon, he never stopped brooding over "the Valley." The activities of the American millionaire Theodore Davis, who held the concession to dig there, were widely reported. Carter followed Davis's excavations step by step as numerous tombs were uncovered, some royal, some not, all plundered in antiquity with one exception: the almost intact tomb of Thuya and Yuya, parents of Queen Tiye. The tomb created a sensation with its fine furniture and perfectly preserved mummies, but it was soda pop next to the champagne of Tut's tomb—which Davis suddenly announced to the world that he had discovered as well.

Imagine that you are Carter. You are in the middle of the complicated excavation of a reused Middle Kingdom tomb (ca. 2000 BC) that has evidence of intrusive burials all the way down the line: fine New Kingdom coffins (ca. 1500 BC) and late dynastic mummies (ca. 900 BC) and piles of Graeco-Roman "junk" (ca. 330 BC–AD 200). It requires all your concentration as you work in the mongrel tomb with its intermingled remains. But how can you keep your mind on Tetiky, ancient mayor of Thebes—or even on Tetiky's unwrapped wife, two mummified miscarriages between her legs, when you hear that that arrogant, careless, filthy rich American had finally gotten the prize you most desired?

Davis was jubilant—he went crowing all over the Valley—now there would be another royal find to his credit! And another one of his lush, expensive, leather-bound publications to announce it. Volumes notoriously and maddeningly short on crucial archaeological detail—Davis had no patience with the vital facts and information compiled by his archaeologists—and equally notoriously and maddeningly long on "modest" bows by the immodest Davis. And in fact *The Tombs of Harmhabi and Toutânkhamanou* (*The*

Tombs of Horemheb and Toutankhamun) by Theodore Davis was just such a work—glossy, flashy, vain, and, archaeologically speaking, useless.

Davis was triumphant—while Carter was left with what, after years of calculation? A hatched map showing the area where Tut's tomb must be, a triangle formed by three royal tombs that Carter had marked out with a firm, experienced hand:

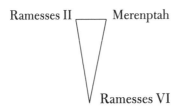

Ramesses II ⎯⎯ Merenptah

Ramesses VI

Which was just where that damned Davis found him.

But then Carter learned the details. The tomb (given the number 58) was one room—a naked little rough chamber barely five feet by four and six feet in depth. Surely it was not a royal tomb, Carter decided.

Surely it was, Davis announced, shrugging off its unroyal proportions: The insignificant boy Tut, son of a despised heretic, would not have been given a grand burial. Among other evidence in the tomb, a strip of thick gold foil had been found, gilding torn off a royal chariot. Tut's figure was engraved on the foil, riding in a chariot and shooting arrows at a target to which foreign captives were bound.

There was no mistaking the cartouche with Tut's throne name inscribed in the middle—the basket for Neb, or "Lord of"; the dung beetle for Kheperure, or "Manifestation of" (literally: "Becoming"); and the disk for Ra, or "Sun": Nebkheperure, Lord of the Sun's Manifestation.

Davis announced that now everything that was to be found in

the Valley had been found. He "fears the Valley is now exhausted," as he put it, and he gave up the now worthless concession.

Which Carter tried to convince Carnarvon to take up. Carnarvon hesitated. A long list of experts agreed with Davis—the Valley had been "done." The consensus of archaeological opinion was against Carter; and even Maspero, renowned for his scholarship, suggested that Carnarvon would do better to dig elsewhere.

Carter insisted that Davis was wrong, that the gold foil with Tut's name was not original to the tomb. It had most probably been carried in by later flooding, he argued. Every instinct told him that #58 was not a royal burial, but an ordinary pit tomb like nearby #54, also stumbled upon by Davis some years earlier.

At the time, Davis had attached no importance to #54 with its meager contents: satchels of a mineral used in embalming (natron), earthenware pots, mummy bandages, and floral wreaths thrown together with bones from an ancient funeral feast. Davis had torn to bits some of the floral wreaths at a dinner party and given away the worthless find for the asking—the asker being Herbert Winlock of New York's Metropolitan Museum of Art, who wanted to take the objects back to America for further study (the find can still be seen in a small room in the Met).

But if Davis was not interested in the undramatic contents of #54, Carter was. He noted the Eighteenth Dynasty pots (Petrie's training) and took to heart Winlock's opinion that the material had been used in a royal burial. In addition, Carter pointed out to Carnarvon that a green faience cup bearing Tut's name had been found behind a boulder in "the triangle."

If Davis was wrong and Tut's tomb still remained to be discovered, and if Tut was in fact buried in the Valley (as the embalming cache and faience cup seemed to indicate), then, Carter argued, there was a good chance it was unplundered. He pointed to the lists of the ancient priests of Amun who had overseen the royal necropolis. During Ramesside times, they had recorded the royal tombs that had been broken into, the royal burials that had to be "renewed"—Carter could reel them off by heart and knew that Tutankhamun's name was not among them.

Carnarvon took his time deciding. Once he backed Carter, he would back him all the way, but it was daunting to put up a fortune—not to mention being thought a fool by those in the know—on the basis of some old mummy rags and lists drawn up by priests three thousand years ago. Any day a donkey's leg could go through the ground and in some underground cache or other another ancient list of plundered tombs might be found with Tutankhamun's name on top.

Davis was preparing his volumes on Tut's tomb; Maspero—who had recommended Carter to begin with—disagreed with Carter. Other archaeologists had tried to interest Carnarvon in digging elsewhere—why remain in the much-explored Valley when better results might be achieved elsewhere?

But stay in the Valley Carnarvon did. Each reason he gave himself against remaining was an added incentive to remain as well. After all, Carnarvon was a sportsman, and what real sportsman could resist backing a dark horse? He agreed to take the concession, and now at last the way was open for Carter to test his cherished theory. Only one obstacle remained to be gotten over, and then he could begin—World War I.

When war was declared, Carter reported for duty in Cairo, where he was assigned to the Department of Military Information. The menace was not just in Europe, but right across Egypt's borders; for Palestine was part of the Ottoman Empire, which had sided with the Central Powers and declared war on Great Britain. The Suez Canal must be protected if the Allies were to win, and desert scouts with a good knowledge of Arabic were in demand.

But there was more to Carter than his expert knowledge of the terrain. There was his nervousness, his poor temper, his bad manners, his inability to get along with most people. After a short stint with the government, Carter was discharged from the service, the War Administration deciding they were better off without him.

For Carter, World War I meant that he had time on his hands. Now he had the leisure to get his teeth fixed and to scour Cairo's markets, where because of the war antiquities were going for a song.

We next see him in the teeming Cairo railroad station. Making his way through the crowds of soldiers setting out to guard the canal, he was heading in the opposite direction. For soon after his discharge, Carter headed back to Luxor, where Carnarvon had built him a home: Simple, domed in Arabic style, constructed with bricks from a foundry Carnarvon owned in England, it was situated on a desert mound overlooking the Valley of the Kings.

What did Cairo have to offer him? Though he and Carnarvon could not yet make use of the Valley concession, still this was the place where he belonged. If the war had any impact on Carter, it was only in terms of the tombs, specifically a tomb in the lonely valley Wadi e 'Tăqa e 'Zeide.

As he told the story (which throws a unique light on the Theban necropolis during wartime): "The absence of officials owing to the war, to say nothing of the general demoralization caused by the war itself, had naturally created a great revival of activity on the part of the local native tomb robbers, and prospecting parties [of thieves] were out in all directions.

"News came into the village one afternoon that a find had been made in an unfrequented region on the western side of the mountain above The Valley of the Kings. Immediately a rival party of diggers armed themselves and made their way to the spot, and in the lively engagement that ensued the original party were beaten and driven off, vowing vengeance.

"To avert further trouble the notables of the village came to me and asked me to take action. It was already late in the afternoon, so I hastily collected the few of my workmen who had escaped the

Army Labour Levies, and with the necessary materials set out for the scene of action, an expedition involving a climb of more than 1,800 feet over the Kurna [Gurneh] hills by moonlight. It was midnight when we arrived on the scene, and the guide pointed out to me the end of a rope which dangled sheer down the face of a cliff.

"Listening, we could hear the robbers actually at work, so I first severed their rope, thereby cutting off their means of escape, and then, making secure a good stout rope of my own, I lowered myself down the cliff. Shinning down a rope at midnight, into a nestful of industrious tomb robbers, is a pastime which at least does not lack excitement.

"There were eight at work, and when I reached the bottom there was an awkward moment. I gave them the alternative of clearing out by means of my rope, or else of staying where they were without a rope at all, and eventually they saw reason and departed. The rest of the night I spent on the spot, and as soon as it was light enough, climbed down into the tomb again to make a thorough examination."

After a difficult clearance with a small team of men (the work financed by Carnarvon), the tomb was found to be an early one of Queen Hatshepsut's, empty of all but a beautiful quartzite sarcophagus—which, however, the Service des Antiquités' tough new director, Pierre Lacau, would not allow Carnarvon to keep.

Gaston Maspero had just retired at the end of a long and distinguished career, worn out not only by the strains of the directorship, but by the death of his son. Arthur Weigall related that when Maspero visited Luxor, all he wanted to do was play with Weigall's children; his heart was no longer in his work. (In a few years' time, Weigall too would be "out of the business": Suffering a nervous breakdown, he would return to London to write potboilers and design exotic stage sets.)

Had Maspero continued as director, Carnarvon certainly would have been recompensed with the sarcophagus. But times were changing, and Carter was caught between the old and the new. Lacau had taken over the service with the firm intention of retaining everything discovered for Egypt; further, he planned on giving institutions of learning precedence over private excavation teams—such as Carter and Carnarvon's.

CHAPTER 13

T HE SARCOPHAGUS WAS AN INDICATION OF WHAT WAS TO COME
when Carter faced the great task of his life: Once Tut's
tomb was opened, Pierre Lacau goaded and insulted Carter
like a toreador prodding a mad bull. He not only denied the
Carnarvon/Carter team a division of the spoils, but refused him
permission even to show the tomb to a party of his colleagues'
wives, thus forcing a showdown, which by that point was what he
wanted, to bring their quarrel out into the open.

From today's point of view, Lacau's resistance to the
Carnarvon/Carter team is perfectly natural; but it must be remembered that at the time of the tomb's opening, Carter had been digging with Carnarvon for sixteen years, working in good faith under
an agreement established at the very beginning.

He would not agree that Lacau or anyone else had the right suddenly, at the moment of his success, to change the rules. He would
not give in to national passions, to Lacau's scientific slogans, or to
the newspaper campaigns. The tomb would be closed for two
years while he fought a losing battle. And he became a kind of sacred monster—isolated after Carnarvon's death, heroic, villainous,
with a strange, "affected" voice that talked familiarly about the
long, long dead.

At this point, however, the new director did not yet show his
hand. Even under the old rules, unique pieces were reserved for

the Egyptian Museum: Carter and Carnarvon did not consider the piece they found in Wadi e 'Táqa e 'Zeide to be unique. But Lacau declared that the thirty-five-hundred-year-old royal monument must remain in Egypt, and he was the last court of appeal in the matter.

Though the issue rankled, it was forgotten as the war drew to a close and the Carter/Carnarvon team prepared to dig at last in the Valley of the Kings itself. Carter's plan was to clear the area he had marked out down to bedrock. Mountains of debris from earlier excavations were scattered about, so there was only one way to ascertain what was really underneath: to clear it all away, foot by foot if necessary.

Which it proved to be. During the first season, nothing was found. Likewise, season number two brought rien—nicht—nothing, giving the international community its first good laugh since the war. A colleague, Arthur Mace, tried to comfort the forlorn team as their third and then fourth futile seasons rolled by: Archaeology, he intoned, is like a second marriage—the triumph of hope over experience.

But Carter and Carnarvon were way past their "second" marriage—they were on their way to outdoing Elizabeth Taylor, going into their sixth marriage (that is, season), with nothing more to show for it than a dozen or so Ramesses II alabaster vases finally dug out of the rubble (by Lady Carnarvon, who, atypically, had decided to desert her lover for a spell). It was a measure of the vases' insignificance that Lacau let the explorers keep whichever ones they wanted.

Carnarvon returned empty-handed to Highclere Castle, where perhaps the bracing cold or the gloomy, misty fields cleared his head. He realized that the whole venture was insane, doomed, and going to bankrupt the noble house of Carnarvon.

Carter had returned to England as well to help his first patron, William Tyssen-Amherst, who was having money troubles as well (in a few years, he would go bankrupt). Just now, however, Carter had been asked to help him sell off some pieces from Tyssen-Amherst's Egyptian collection; he was to act as Tyssen-Amherst's agent with Sotheby's (first to go: the large granite statues of Sekhmet, the lion-headed goddesses who had awed the boy Carter on his way to sketch the family pets).

Hearing that Carter was in England, Carnarvon invited him to Highclere for a talk, determined to call it a day.

An account of their interview was given to us by James Breasted, one of the first American Egyptologists and founder of the University of Chicago's Oriental Institute. Carter's contemporary and co-worker, Breasted was one of the few colleagues with whom Carter remained on good terms for his whole life. (Of course, they had a falling-out: Carter bought an antiquity to which Breasted claimed he had right of first refusal. But it was nothing in the scheme of Carter's violent quarrels with almost everyone.)

Breasted was someone to whom Carter turned in a pinch—when Tut's tomb was discovered, for instance, Breasted immediately showed up and generously gave of his epigraphic expertise, recording and deciphering the many seals plastered over its walls and doors. His account of the Carnarvon-Carter meeting, therefore, was to be trusted.

"In the summer of 1922," Breasted revealed, "after still another unsuccessful season of excavation, Carnarvon summoned him to Highclere Castle to discuss the question of whether they should continue this expensive and thus far fruitless task. Carnarvon rather dreaded the interview which as it then seemed to him could end only in a decision even more saddening for Carter, if possible, than for himself. . . .

"Carter also anticipated their interview with anxiety, for he better than anyone knew that thus far the record warranted no other conclusion. His one hope resided in a simple plan which he proposed to lay before Carnarvon.

"When they finally met at Highclere, Carnarvon reviewed the history of their work, expressed again his appreciation of the years of effort Carter had given to it, and with genuine regret stated that in view of the post war economic stringency, he would find it impossible to support further this obviously barren undertaking.

"In reply Carter said that their consistent failure to find anything had not in the slightest weakened the conviction he had held for years, that The Valley contained *at least* one more royal tomb—" Italics mine. This at least is really something. It sets Carter apart. What is he saying! Not only is King Tut buried in the Valley, but there may be other undiscovered royal tombs as well! And he has the chutzpah to offer this opinion after so many hundreds of thousands of pounds have been wasted.

He followed this up with another gesture that was quite wonderful, a kind of grand shrug: "He granted that perhaps even this problematical tomb might have been robbed in antiquity—"

What is Carter "granting"?! That even if they find Tut's tomb, it may be empty! One can just imagine Carnarvon mopping his brow or jumping up and turning the portrait of his father, the Fourth Earl of Carnarvon, to the wall, for surely in the history of Highclere Castle the family's cash assets had never been squandered so recklessly. Horses, mistresses, and marathon card games were solid investments compared with this.

Whatever Carnarvon's reaction, he let Carter finish his spiel: Granted, Carter said as if he were the lord and Carnarvon the retainer, granted it all might be for nothing, it might be that the tomb had been robbed in antiquity—but then again—Carter wound up: "There was always the possibility that it had not!"

Now, admittedly words were not Carter's strong suit. One of his colleagues (Breasted) put it a little strongly, perhaps, when he wrote in a letter, "It is well known that Carter does not know the meaning of the English language." Fine—he was a practical man, a sharp-eyed observer of nature, a craftsmanlike artist, a great drafts-man, a good photographer, an intuitive, practically self-taught ar-chaeologist, and he was in a class by himself as an excavator. What did it matter that he wasn't eloquent?

Ghostwriters and collaborators helped him cook up his ac-count of the discovery of Tut's tomb—comparing it with his let-ters, excavation reports, and the like, one can easily spot what an act of ventriloquism his popular (and profitable) writings were. Ditto his lectures. Say of Carter (as Madame de Staël said of one of her lovers), "Speech is not his language!"

Still, surely Carter could have come up with a better conclusion than this when arguing his case before Carnarvon, some moving speech, some clinching syllogism, some eloquent appeal. How-ever, Hermes Trismegistus help him, he did not.

What did Carter do next? Breasted tells us that he "laid before him [Carnarvon] the familiar map—" The map! One can imagine what a welcome sight that was to Carnarvon, who had seen it so often that he could have shown it to Carter by this time. The map, "which recorded, season by season, the account of their probing and excavation. At first glance, not a square metre of Valley floor and slopes appeared unchecked, but Carter reminded him that just below the entrance to the tomb of Rameses VI there remained a small triangular area—" The triangle again! Another sight that must have been most welcome to Carnarvon's eyes.

And why had Carter left it until last, this wonderful triangle of his? Why for the last six years had he ignored the place of his orig-inal hunch, the area where Theodore Davis had found his King Tut's tomb, the place where Edward Ayrton had reached behind a boulder to find the telltale green faience cup with Tut's name? What had he been waiting for? The answer he gave reminds one of a derelict schoolboy excusing his unpreparedness: He was waiting for an opportune moment!

What is he talking about? "Some later, off-season time because it would temporarily prevent visitors from entering the foregoing tomb." That is, the tomb of Ramesses VI.

Now, this sounds simply beyond belief, and more than one Egyptologist has questioned it. Not only wild-eyed weavers of conspiracy theories (of whom there are many), but a clear-eyed, learned, lucid, and interesting scholar such as Christine El Mahdy—for one—doesn't believe Carter for a minute. An Egyptologist at Yeovil College, England, she has pursued a lifelong interest in King Tut by carefully and critically studying all the available evidence.

In her thought-provoking *Tutankhamen,* she underscores her skepticism by pointing out, quite correctly, that as inspector, Carter had worked on strengthening the retaining wall leading to the entrance of Ramesses VI's tomb. That means he would have been working directly over the entrance to Tut's tomb. How can one believe he didn't know about it? No, she opines, he knew it, but he was saving it for just such a moment as this: It was his ace in the hole for when Carnarvon should get tired of bankrolling a fruitless series of digs at high price.

Why should Carter have proceeded in this way? Well, unfortunately, one such doubt leads to another—and another and another—until we see Carter as either the mastermind of a complicated plot unequaled in the annals of archaeology—or a fool!

Was he looting the tomb through secret entrances running into it from below, behind, or on the side (another theory proposed by less scrupulous theorists than Mahdy)? Did he have a fleet of airplanes hovering overhead to take away the treasure, as was widely believed not only by the villagers, but even by sober members of the Wafd (or Nationalist) Party? Did he—

But wait! Let us draw back from these crazy theories and return to the well-informed Ms. Mahdy (whose account of Tutankhamun's tomb is filled with truly striking, original, and thought-provoking insights). It is possible that she is right that Carter knew about Tut's tomb from the beginning, but Carter's motive—or rather his motive behind his motive—is not convincing.

Say he wanted to string Carnarvon along (motive number one, given by Mahdy). But why? Why is he buying time? One has to answer that—and in doing so, one falls into a morass of speculation that just does not jibe with something essential to Carter: For whatever fetishes, dishonesties, rages, and out-and-out craziness he was capable of, he had integrity in the higher sense.

The (literally) thousands of painstakingly accurate index cards he filled out in his clearance of Tut's tomb; the fanatically detailed sketches of objects; the care with which he treated the rotting cloth and fragile wooden antiquities of the tomb; the fanaticism with which he polished the jewelry and restored every atom of the royal chariots—down to the gilded horse blinkers—all was a result of his love for his work, his genius, his devotion.

Did he give in to dark impulses? Certainly! Did he try to steal this or that? Without a doubt. Was he a part of some Mafia-style scam? It seems to the present writer that the answer is an emphatic no.

It is altogether possible to say that Carter's digging away from Tut's tomb when he was just within a few feet of it at the very beginning is altogether in the nature of things. There is an irony about the way the world is put together, as thinkers from the Egyptian Old Kingdom on have observed.

After the fact, one can exclaim with disbelief: How is it possible? But one would perhaps have to be out in the hot sun surrounded by rubble and singing workers to enter into Carter's feverish gambler's frame of mind. One would have to hear the laughter of his colleagues, to feel the insult of his dismissal as inspector, and to have had the experience of years in dark, claustrophobic tombs to know just what motivated Carter to act this way or that. And as the simplest explanation is the one generally accepted in the scientific model, perhaps one should resort to simplicity as well in accounting for human motives.

Breasted continued his account of the Carnarvon-Carter meeting: "In this area," Carter explains to Carnarvon, referring to the "triangle," "he [Carter] had noted the foundation remains of a row of crude stone huts, evidently built by ancient tomb workmen, which he would have to remove in order to probe the terrain beneath them."

Just what these ancient crude stone huts were must be explained. During the unstable last days of the Eighteenth Dynasty, Ay seized for himself the large, royal-size tomb that had been excavated in the West Valley—probably the one originally intended for Tut—and buried the boy-king in a tomb that had probably been dug for some high-placed but nonroyal aristocrat.

Ay did not live long, and his successor, General Horemheb, had no children, passing the throne along to a fellow soldier, Ramesses I, who founded the Nineteenth Dynasty. Which in turn was followed by a long line of Ramesses in the Twentieth Dynasty.

This was what preserved Tut for three millennia—that the Ramessides built over the relatively small tomb (small by Eighteenth Dynasty royal standards: a flight of sixteen steps, a corridor, an antechamber with a side room, or "annex," on one side, a sealed door on the other leading to the burial chamber, with another storeroom, the treasury, to one side). Ramesses VI's tomb was just a little higher up on the slope; and the Ramesside tomb workers also covered up the forgotten boy-king's sepulcher with their huts.

Huts that Carter now proposed to demolish as he laid his cards on the table. Breasted concluded, "Now, said Carter, only when this triangle had been cleared would he feel that their work in The Valley had been absolutely completed. He therefore wished to propose that Carnarvon grant him permission to undertake one more season's work at his—Carter's—own expense, using Carnarvon's concession, and the same workmen and equipment he had employed for years; and if at the end of this final season he found nothing, he would of course, and with a good conscience, agree that they should abandon The Valley.

"But if on the other hand he should make a discovery, it should belong to Carnarvon exactly as under their long-standing arrangement. . . .

"Carter's proposal appealed to him [Carnarvon] as eminently fair—in fact, as too generous. He would agree, he said, to another and final season of excavation; but it would be at his own, not Carter's expense. . . ."

Poor Carnarvon! Oppressed by "post war stringencies" and heavy expenses! Burdened by a huge estate and a small army of old family servants and pensioners! The sole support of an extravagant wife and her indigent lover! Obliged to underwrite a famous stable and an infamous archaeologist—a fanatical excavator who was either a genius or a fool, who held out to him crumbling earthenware pots and torn linen bandages as a sure sign of treasure!

Poor Carnarvon, everyone had a hand in his pocket! He was shelling out left and right at a time when my lord of this was renting out his castle and my lady of that was going bankrupt—take the Tyssen-Amhersts, selling off their Sekhmets, a terrible business.

But he had given his word, and he did not go back on it. He stood the test. At a time when he did not know where his next plate of pâté de foie gras was coming from, he backed Carter on a final throw of the dice.

CHAPTER 14

EVERYTHING HAPPENED VERY QUICKLY AFTER THIS MEETING at Highclere—with such speed that Carter barely had the chance to catch his breath. It was as if they had to be tested first—each according to his capabilities—before the earth would open up under their feet and yield up what they had been seeking.

Toward the end of October, Carter returned to Luxor and told his reis to round up the workers—there would be another season after all. Then he strode out to the site to plan and record the ancient workers' huts, which must first of all be torn down (at least those beneath Ramesses VI's tomb). If he had been "sleepwalking" around this vital area before, now he was wide awake.

There was a layer of rubble under the huts, around three feet deep, and by November 3 the men began to clear this away, preparing to trench toward the south of the triangle.

But before they got very far, a young water boy, hired the day before, saw a step beneath the soil and cried out. Though sometimes Carter mentioned him in his lectures, in his written account the boy did not appear. Except for varying details such as this, Carter's written account can be trusted (at least until he reaches the inner door). Indeed, it would be very difficult for him to depart from the truth, since every step of his way into the tomb was so closely watched.

"Hardly had I arrived on the work next morning," he wrote,

"than the unusual silence, due to the stoppage of the work, made me realize that something out of the ordinary had happened . . . a step cut in the rock had been discovered underneath the very first hut to be attacked. This seemed too good to be true, but a short amount of extra clearing revealed the fact that we were actually in the entrance of a steep cut in the rock. . . ."

It seemed too good to be true not only to Carter, but to skeptics who read his story. But if this sudden discovery was a "setup," as has been suggested, surely Carter would have been more clever about it. He would have waited a month or at least a few weeks before "allowing" the discovery to take place. In any case, the nervous strain Carter suffered until the tomb was finally opened was evident to everyone who knew him. Far from being assured, he was like a man on trial for his life. He could not sleep, he could not eat, he could not stop speculating about what he had found—a cache or a tomb, an intact burial or an empty, plundered sepulcher.

The men had to keep digging, since "masses of rubbish overlay the cut." They cleared step after step until finally they were positive it was a descending staircase they were working on. Carter stood rooted to the spot, watching until finally by the twelfth step the men reached "the upper part of a doorway, blocked, plastered, and sealed."

The seal gave no clue as to the owner's identity. It was the jackal over nine captives seal used by necropolis officials. Clearly whoever was buried here was of importance, but nothing more could be inferred. Carter hollowed out a peephole, but the passageway behind the door was filled in with rubble.

"Anything, literally anything, might lie beyond that passage," he wrote, "and it needed all my self control to keep from breaking down the doorway and investigating then and there."

But it was late in the day, and the sun was beginning to set. Clearing the passageway behind the door would take time. Its rubble must be sifted for possible clues, and Carter was a professional.

He might break the service's rules, but he would never jeopardize the smallest scrap of knowledge to be gleaned from a find. Petrie had trained him too well for that.

Again, he was tortured by doubts. If it was Tut's tomb, why was the entranceway so narrow? The necropolis seals were a good sign—but then, they didn't necessarily prove anything. There might be nothing at the end of that passageway but a bundle of bones stripped of jewelry and amulets and reburied in antiquity by pious ancient priests.

If he had cleared away just a few more inches of rubble, if he had exposed just a little more of the lower part of the door, he would have found Tutankhamun's royal seal as well. But that did not happen. For security, the workmen shoveled back all the debris onto the steps and then rolled huge flint boulders in front of its entrance. Carter's reis bedded down for the night in front of the tomb, together with his most trusted men. And then Carter rode home through the moonlit desert.

The next day, he telegraphed Carnarvon, who was in England, "At last have made wonderful discovery in valley: a magnificent tomb with seals intact; recovered same for your arrival; congratulations." Then he must sit back and wait—he owed it to his patron to do nothing until he arrived.

He had overstated the matter in his telegram, as critics point out. But what could be more natural? After so many years of pursuing Tut, of course he was carried away by the possibility of success. In any case, he was not the only one to be carried away. When Carnarvon appeared two weeks later with his young daughter, Lady Evelyn, there was electricity in the air. The province's governor escorted them from the train with a guard of honor while crowds cheered, though of course, nothing was certain yet.

The boulders were rolled away, the staircase was cleared, and this time with the entire doorway uncovered, Tut's seals could be clearly seen. But a new element was added. An examination of the seals on the doorway made it clear that the portion of the door bearing the necropolis seal had been opened twice and resealed twice.

"Plunderers had entered it, and entered it more than once," Carter realized. "But that they had not rifled it completely was evident from the fact that it had been resealed." There was no way of knowing, of course, and the tension built as Carter, with Carnarvon looking over his shoulder, proceeded with the work.

On November 25, they removed the blocking stones from the doorway and found that the corridor behind it was completely filled in with stone and rubble. Again, there was evidence of plundering: A tunnel had been dug through the filling. Clearing this passageway took up the rest of the day, but by the next morning, they had reached a second, inner door. The moment of truth had arrived.

"With trembling hands I made a tiny breach in the upper left hand corner," Carter wrote. "Darkness and blank space, as far as an iron testing rod could reach, showed that whatever lay beyond was empty and not filled like the passage we had just cleared . . . and then, widening the hole a little, I inserted the candle and peered in. Lord Carnarvon, Lady Evelyn and Callender standing anxiously beside me to hear the verdict.

"At first I could see nothing, the hot air escaping from the chamber causing the candle flame to flicker, but presently, as my eyes grew accustomed to the light, details of the room within emerged slowly from the mist, strange animals, statues and gold—everywhere the glint of gold. For the moment—an eternity it must have seemed to the others standing by—I was struck dumb with amazement, and when Lord Carnarvon, unable to stand the suspense any longer, inquired anxiously, 'Can you see anything?' it was all I could do to get out the words, 'Yes, wonderful things.' "

Carter's whole life was a preparation for this moment—but nothing could prepare him for what he saw—a sudden burst of fantasy sixteen steps beneath the stark desert cliffs. For the splendor of Tut's tomb partook more of the realm of the imaginary than the real. He stepped through Alice's looking-glass into a room filled with casket after casket of fantastic jewelry, gilded couches, and brilliantly beaded clothing, chariots, and fans and boats and vases—the list is staggering.

But what he saw when he stood there peering through the hole was just a fraction of the find. He recorded that his exhilaration gave way to solemnity when he actually entered the tomb and saw that the antechamber led to three more rooms filled with astonishing works of art and fragile antiquities. He fell silent, realizing that the tomb was more than a wonderful find. It was a responsibility and a burden that by the end would consume the rest of his life.

In the larger sense, Carter's story ends here. The excavator passed King Tut on that stairway of sixteen finely chiseled steps. Tut was resurrected after thirty-three centuries. He came alive in scene after scene from the tomb. His features, serene and noble, molded in gold, entered modern consciousness as an icon of the past.

While Carter, the main quest of his life fulfilled, descended into the tomb as surely as if he were wrapped in linen winding bandages. Of course, there would be lectures, banquets, political struggles, the work of restoration. He would be insulted, enraged—and he would dine with presidents and kings. But for all that, the rest of his life was one long postscript to this moment of revelation that left him speechless with wonder.

EPILOGUE

The main hall of the Egyptian Museum.
LIBRARY OF CONGRESS

THE REAL CURSE OF TUT'S TOMB WAS THAT CARTER DID NOT die at the moment of discovery.

After decades of working in solitude and silence, suddenly Carter found himself in the midst of a circus. His old enemy Arthur Weigall, now reporting for the *Daily Mail,* described the scene: "There were soldiers springing to the salute; officers with clanking swords shouting orders; Cinema operators running up the hillsides, while native boys climbed behind them carrying their apparatus; crowds of European and American visitors in every kind of costume from equestrian to regatta; Egyptian notables looking very hot in western clothes and red tarboushes; tall black eunuchs in frock coats; and dragomans [guides] in bright silken robes...."

The world's spotlight was suddenly turned on Carter—and at the worst possible moment. For as the ancient air rushed out of the tomb and the modern air entered, the process of decay and destruction began—and would have to be countered as soon as possible. James Breasted recorded that as he sat deciphering seals in the tomb, "strange rustling murmuring whispering sounds rose and fell and died away.... The outside air had altered the temperature and quality of atmosphere, causing the wood to adjust to new strains. Hence the audible snapping and fracturing [of the antiquities]."

Huge amounts of preservatives and packing material had to be brought from Cairo—along with a solid steel door. A laboratory needed to be set up in a neighboring tomb, a photographic record made, and a darkroom established in an empty tomb nearby; draftsmen were necessary to work on a careful plan to scale—a team had to be put together, a chemist found, an engineer, a photographer, and so on, before Carter could take the first steps in clearing the tomb. (The New York Metropolitan Museum of Art, excavating nearby, stepped in right away with generous offers of help.)

But if Carter was in the middle of an archaeological crisis, he was also engulfed by a political one. From day one of the tomb's discovery, nationalists raised the cry: Everything must remain in Egypt! The struggle for independence was at its height now, after World War I, with assassinations, demonstrations, strikes, and the like. British gentlemen could be seen checking their guns as they entered the Gezira Sporting Club—it was unsafe even in Cairo for them to go about unarmed. If the foreign crowds gathered above the tomb *ooh*ed and *aah*ed the overnight celebrities being brought up the tomb's sixteen steps—Anubis, Isis, & Co.—the nationalists claimed the gilded images as their own. These treasures became the symbol of Egypt's reawakening.

The nationalists' demands were echoed by the new director of the Antiquities Service, Pierre Lacau, who also wanted the tomb's contents to remain in Egypt, though for reasons of his own. He called for an end to the old rule of "partage," or division. A scattering of Egypt's treasures on the art markets and in private collections impeded scientific study, he claimed with some justice. But his motives were mixed, with jealousy and ambition playing their part in his intrigues against Carter.

He was quick to use a legal argument against the excavators: The contents of an intact royal tomb belonged entirely to the Egyptian government, according to the never before invoked terms of Carnarvon's concession. Carnarvon pointed out that Tut's tomb had been robbed in antiquity and thus was not intact. "Rifled" was a better word for it, Lacau countered. True, unguents, perfumes, and jewelry had been stolen—but Tut's mummy had been left undisturbed, Lacau insisted.

From the beginning, this fact had been more or less certain. At the grand opening of the burial chamber, a huge gilded wooden shrine was seen to take up most of the room. When its doors were slowly folded back, the seals on a second, inner shrine were found intact. As it turned out, there were four gilded shrines covering the royal sarcophagus, and as soon as the unbroken seals on the second shrine were noted, it was understood that the body of the boy-king had not been touched.

Later, when the shrines were finally dismantled and the two-ton sarcophagus cover was lifted, this surmise was proven correct: Tut was found lying in a nest of three "anthropoid," or portrait, coffins, each one more exquisite than the last. The inner one was of solid gold and contained yet another amazing image of Tut, a gold portrait mask of unsurpassed beauty.

Carnarvon had no intention of letting the matter rest at this. He had laid out huge sums during the unprofitable sixteen years of financing Carter's digs (the last six years alone had cost him over forty-five thousand English pounds). If he had to, he would subpoena Tut himself to win his case.

His share of the find in question, Carnarvon devoted the last six weeks of his life to figuring out how to make back some of his money. He negotiated with both Cinema Pathé and MGM for film rights, delighted with an MGM scenario starring a heroic earl. He sold exclusive photos to newspapers, journals, and collectors and advised Carter to paint "some really good piece" from the tomb, telling him that he would be able to sell it at a very high price. (Another irritating suggestion from his oblivious lordship, who, unlike Carter, had no sense of the difficulty and delicacy of the work ahead.)

Of all Carnarvon's moneymaking schemes, though, the one that would hang like an albatross around Carter's neck was the exclusive (for a hefty sum) the earl granted the London *Times.* From the beginning, the needy nobleman saw that the three-thousand-year-old pharaoh was hot news. The story made headlines right away and stayed on the first page as day by day the hysteria grew: KING'S VISCERA GUARDED BY FOUR GOLDEN GODDESSES! QUEEN OF THE BELGIANS ARRIVES FOR TOMB'S OPENING! WILL TUT HIMSELF BE FOUND? And so on.

The world could not get enough of Tut—even before Carnarvon's death created absolute pandemonium—the curse!—with psychics and necromancers of every sort grabbing the limelight. The earl was laid to rest amid a chorus of dire predictions about those still working in the tomb, the foremost being, of course, the unbelieving, "arrogant" Howard Carter.

But while the psychics might give interviews free of charge, any news given to the reporters descending on Luxor would have to be bought from the *Times*—an arrangement that included the Egyptian press, who were treated as foreigners in their own land. The reporting was, accordingly, hostile to Carnarvon and Carter, with Weigall in the front of the hunting pack, inventing freely, maliciously, stirring up as much animosity toward the "monopolists" as possible.

Even under the best of circumstances, Carter was not a man to shrug off such attacks. But now they were magnified times ten, Carter being in the midst of delicate archaeological work. As temperatures climbed toward the end of the work season—100 degrees, 105, 110, 120—Carter was to be found working on his knees in the airless tomb, or hanging from a sling over the treasures in the annex, a room packed so solidly that it was impossible to walk safely among its vases and chests.

With Carnarvon dead, Carter was shouldering the full burden of public relations as well as the delicate, all-consuming archaeological work: His nerves were on edge, and he was particularly vulnerable to Lacau, who had been carrying on a campaign of petty annoyances and restrictions all along. Finally, Lacau made his move. Informed that Carter planned on inviting the wives of his collaborators to view the tomb, Lacau sent an order from Cairo forbidding this.

Not considering that he was walking into a trap, Carter closed the tomb in a rage and posted Lacau's letter at the Winter Palace Hotel as a public denunciation of Lacau and the Egyptian government's discourtesy, incompetence, and interference. Lacau immediately canceled the Carnarvon concession and sent in government officials to change the locks, claiming that Carter had abandoned his duty at a critical moment and thus no longer had a right to work in the tomb.

Thus began the saga of lawsuits and political wrangling that would end some two years later in defeat—inevitably, for Lacau and the Egyptian government held all the cards.

After losing his case in the mixed courts (so called from its makeup of both European and Egyptian officials), Carter appealed. While fruitless negotiations were carried on, locked out of "his" tomb, he left for a speaking tour in the United States and Canada.

If there is one image that sums up Carter during this time, it is a scene that took place on the Canadian Pacific Railway, in the dining car of the Montreal–Ottawa train. The steward handed the world-famous explorer the menu, and according to Lee Keedick, his speaker's agent, Carter frantically filled in the "patron's comments" section with sarcastic, biting criticisms, going on to cover the entire bill of fare in his fine, precise handwriting.

But this was typical of Carter's last phase: embattled, bitter, futile. When he finally returned to spend a decade in the tomb, it was after signing an apology and humbly accepting the new terms imposed by the Antiquities Service and Egyptian government. Apart from renouncing (for the Carnarvon estate) any share in the tomb's contents and accepting government supervision, he would be forced to wait every morning for a government official to hand him the keys to the tomb—he was no longer allowed to hold them.

A colleague, Gertrude Caton-Thompson, wrote of a visit made during the last decade of clearing: "We found him [Carter] repairing some of the coffin cases; he showed us the multitude of things still awaiting attention and I pitied him cooped up for years in the electrified darkness of the tomb."

During these last years, Carter, walking in the desert, peered through his binoculars and caught a glimpse of an unusual sight: "a pair of jackals . . . making their way towards the cultivated land."

He described them in his journal: "They probably had cubs in the hills as otherwise it was early for them to descend to inhabited and cultivated quarters. But the great interest was, while one of them was of normal size and colouring, the other . . . was totally black, much taller and attenuated, resembling . . . the type found upon the monuments. This is the first example of that colouring and that type of jackal I have seen in Egypt in over thirty five years experience in the desert and it suggested to me the old and original Egyptian jackal, known to us as Anubis, god of the dead."

It was fitting that at the end of his career, these divine zoological throwbacks appeared to Carter. For during the course of his life, he had become just as much a part of Egypt's past as they were. The era that had begun in the early 1800s with adventurers of every imaginable sort pillaging Egypt's ruins ended with the tortured, sensitive, moody Carter. During his lifetime, Egyptology began to take its place among the scientific disciplines, leaving behind its "unrespectable" piratical origins.

The study of Egypt's past has since become more specialized. DNA testing of a lock of hair and a more accurate understanding of the ancient language have taken the place of the search for treasure.

But who knows? There is no ruling out what still may be found! For as Carter wrote, in archaeology it is generally the unexpected that happens.

The same divine jackals that Carter met still circle in the Valley of the Kings—they must, for the gods are eternal, are they not? Possibly they have their own plans for some student setting out to study Egypt's past—from a strictly scientific point of view, mind you. Conceivably, it will be one of you reading this book. For though you may be no lady or gent, jackals have their own way of judging such matters and may decide to lead you to the tomb of some nobleman or noblewoman, some Mitannian or Hittite princess come to Egypt long ago.

Or perhaps they will bless (and damn!) you with an even greater find. The tomb of Ramesses VIII, say—at this moment still lying beneath the shifting sands, waiting to be discovered.

ACKNOWLEDGMENTS

A heartfelt thanks to:

My editor, Jill Schwartzman, for helping to shape the book, for her many insightful suggestions, for her enthusiasm and love of the subject.

My former editor, Nancy Miller, who believed in this book from the first and who kept me going. High intelligence, beauty, and kindness are a rare combination.

My agent, Noah Lukeman, author of *Macbeth II,* for his constant support, encouragement, and interest in my work over the years.

Lea Beresford, who patiently and competently handled the many questions that attended the preparation of this book. It is a pleasure to work with her.

Mary Gow of the Brooklyn Museum's Wilburforce Egyptian Library, whose expertise is staggering (what doesn't this woman know?). Many thanks especially for help with the Hatnub Quarry material.

Adam Lukeman, who, with his art, transformed me in the author's photo.

Berk Straun, for the beautiful and meaningful cover.

Sona Vogel, copy editor with a jeweler's eye, for putting this book through its paces with great care and diligence.

Stephanie Madey, who was very resourceful in tracking down difficult-to-find material for me through a long, hot summer.

For the following friends, without whose help this book could not have been completed: Constance and John Skedgell, Mohsin Rashidi, Mark Roberts, Rosalie Kaufman, Brenda Shoshanna, Leah and Jonathon

Kohn, Princess Ankherut, Vivian Heller, Prof. Maura Spiegel, Prof. Thomas Cohen, Prof. Ross Borden, Jumay Chu, Francine Plavé, Belle Plavé, Charles Mandelbaum, Avi Dov Orzel, Jacob Orzel, Les and Marta Szczygiel, Sylvia Levy, Yoleine Attanas, Helen Auerbach, Goldine Shamas.

NOTES

ABBREVIATIONS

GI: Griffith Institute, Ashmolean Museum, Oxford

MMA: New York Metropolitan Museum of Art

ASAE: *Annales du Service des Antiquités de l'Égypte,* Cairo

PART ONE: EXPENSES PAID AND NOTHING ELSE (BUT FATE)

EPIGRAPH

1 **"Let the one who enters here beware"** Arthur Weigall, *Tutankhamen and Other Essays* (Port Washington, NY/London: Kennikat Press, 1924; reissued 1970), 137. From the tomb of Ursu, mining engineer.

CHAPTER 1

8 **Ironically, it was a harsher method** Joyce Tyldesley, *Judgement of the Pharaoh: Crime and Punishment in Ancient Egypt* (London: Weidenfeld & Nicolson, 2000), 73.

11 **"He was one"** GI, Carter mss., VI.2.1.

11 **"However, if a son"** Ibid.

12 **"I have next to nothing"** Ibid.

12 **"For a living"** Ibid.

14 **"It was the Amherst Egyptian Collection"** Ibid.

14 **"Give him the stick!"** T. E. Peet, *The Great Tomb Robberies of the Twentieth Egyptian Dynasty* (Oxford: Clarendon Press, 1930), 48.

14 **"We went up in a single"** Ibid., 176.

15 **"My father ferried the thieves"** Ibid., 177–180.

16 **"If you come across"** Francis Llewellyn Griffith to John E. New-berry, February 2, 1891, GI, Newberry mss., 1.2/9.

17 **"These venerable people"** GI, Carter mss., VI.2.1.

CHAPTER 2

19 **"a dominant personality"** Emma Andrews diary, January 17, 1902 (Philadelphia: American Philosophical Society): a transcription. Copy in MMA Department of Egyptian Art.

19 **"some scaly, a few furred"** GI, Carter mss., VI.2.1.

20 **"The ground gave way"** Howard Carter, "Report on the Tomb of Mentuhotep 1st, known as Bab El Hosan," *ASAE* 2 (1901): 201–205.

20 **"All that I received"** GI, Carter Notebook 16, 109, quoted in H. V. F. Winstone, *Howard Carter and the Discovery of the Tomb of Tutankhamun* (London: Constable, 1991).

21 **"After working down"** Carter, "Report on the Tomb of Men-tuhotep 1st," 201–205.

22 **"I am hard at work"** Carter to Lady Tyssen-Amherst, Decem-ber 19, 1900, Amherst Letters, in the possession of Dr. Bob Brier, quoted in T.G.H. James, *Howard Carter: The Path to Tut-ankhamun* (Cairo: American University in Cairo Press, 1992), 98.

22 **"Consider the circumstances"** GI, Carter Notebook 5.

24 **"a young excavator"** Ibid.

25 **"gone some way toward"** W. M. Flinders Petrie, *Ten Years' Dig-ging in Egypt: The First Discovery of Tanis, Naukratis, Daphnae and Other Sites* (Chicago: University of Chicago Press, 1989; un-changed reprint, London: Methuen, 1891), 130–132.

25 **"There is the lack"** Ibid.

26 **"The season's work"** Gertrude Caton-Thompson, *Mixed Mem-oirs* (Gateshead: Tyne & Wear, 1922), 84.

26 **"a lowly kingdom"** Ezekiel 29:6–7, 29:14, Nosson Scherman and Meir Zlotowitz, eds., The Chumash [The Hebrew Bible] (Brook-lyn: Mesorah Publications, 1993), 1149.

27 **"I had everything prepared"** GI, Carter Notebook 5, quoted in H.V.F. Winstone, *Howard Carter,* 89.

29 **"I cannot now remember"** Ibid., 90.

29 **"Carter had announced"** Maspero to Naville, January 8, 1901, Archives of the Bibliothèque publique et Universitaire, Geneva, 2529, 223.

30 **With a touch of madness?** Adel Sabit, *A King Betrayed* (London and New York: Quartet, 1989), 99, quoted in Nicholas Reeves and John H. Taylor, *Howard Carter Before Tutankhamun* (London: British Museum Press, 1992), 180.

30 **"Let the one"** Weigall, *Tutankhamen,* 136.

PART TWO: NAKED UNDER AN UMBRELLA

EPIGRAPH

31 **"Archaeology is not a profession"** Margaret Drower, *Flinders Petrie: A Life in Archaeology* (London: Victor Gollancz, 1985), 280.

CHAPTER 3

34 **"emerge just before dawn"** Drower, *Flinders Petrie,* 98.

34 **"I have known him"** Arthur Weigall to Hortense Weigall, undated letter [1901?], Arthur Weigall Archive, quoted in Julie Hankey, *A Passion for Egypt: Arthur Weigall, Tutankhamun and the Curse of the Pharaohs* (London and New York: I. B. Tauris Publishers, 2001), 32.

34 **"Petrie was a man"** Charles Breasted, *Pioneer to the Past: The Story of James H. Breasted* (New York: Charles Scribner's Sons, 1943).

35 **"a man who did not suffer"** GI, Carter mss., VI.2.1, quoted in Reeves and Taylor, *Howard Carter,* 24.

36 **"Exploring on foot"** Caton-Thompson, *Mixed Memoirs,* 84.

36 **"unconsidered trifles"** W. M. Flinders Petrie, *Seventy Years in Archaeology* (London: Methuen, 1931), 19.

37 **"The observation of the small things"** Ibid.

37 **"I traveled here"** James H. Breasted, *Ancient Records of Egypt: Historical Documents,* Vol. I (Chicago: University of Chicago Press, 1906), 212.

38 **"The key to archaeology"** Petrie, *Ten Years' Digging,* 158.

39 "I found him puzzling" GI, Carter mss., VI.2.1, quoted in Reeves and Taylor, *Howard Carter,* 24.

39 **cartonnage** I am indebted to Margaret Drower for her comparison between cartonnage and papier-mâché. Drower, *Flinders Petrie,* 149.

40 **"It is no use"** Petrie journal, January 3–9, 1892, in the Petrie Museum, University College London, cited in James, *Howard Carter,* 36.

40 **"the stealthy convergence of human lots"** George Eliot, *Middlemarch* (New York: Bantam Books, 1985), 85.

41 **"Even the British Museum"** Petrie to Edwards, April 1988, quoted in Drower, *Flinders Petrie,* 138.

CHAPTER 4

44 **"dead men on leave"** Christopher C. Lee, *The Grand Piano Came by Camel: Arthur C. Mace, the Neglected Archaeologist* (Edinburgh: Mainstream Publishing, 1992).

44 **"short, round headed"** Drower, *Flinders Petrie,* 137.

44 **"a procession of gilt mummies"** Ibid., 138, and Leo Deuel, *Memoirs of Heinrich Schliemann: A Documentary Portrait Drawn from His Autobiographical Writings, Letters and Excavation Reports* (New York: Harper & Row, 1977).

45 **"Degradation is followed"** W. M. Flinders Petrie, *Diospolis Parva: The Cemeteries of Abadiyeh and Hu, 1898–9* (London: Egyptian Exploration Fund, 1901).

46 **"It is certainly"** Drower, *Flinders Petrie,* 138.

46 **"one of the greatest applied"** D. G. Kendall, "Some Problems and Methods in Statistical Archaeology," *World Archaeology* I (1969): 68ff. For further elucidation, see "A Statistical Approach to Flinders Petrie's Sequence Dating," *Bulletin of the International Statistical Institute* 40 (1963): 657ff.

47 **"A new scientific truth"** Max Planck, *Scientific Autobiography and Other Papers,* F. Gaynor, trans. (New York: Philosophical Library, 1949), 33–34.

47 **"in the strongest terms"** Drower, *Flinders Petrie,* 138.

47 **"the struggle for existence"** GI, Carter mss., VI.2.1, quoted in Reeves and Taylor, *Howard Carter,* 30.

48 **"smelly dining salon"** Ibid.

49 **Photos of Alexandria in the 1890s** Robert T. Harrison, *Imperialism in Egypt: Techniques of Domination* (Westport, CT, and London: Greenwood Press, 1995). The photos mentioned are from the Huntington Library, San Marino, California, Lady Anna Brassey Collection.

51 **"With our luggage"** GI, Carter mss., VI.2.1.

52 **Eadweard Muybridge** Men Wrestling; Animal Locomotion, plate 345. CF Tomb #13 in Percy Newberry, *Beni Hasan I–IV* (London: Egyptian Exploration Fund Archaeological Survey Memoirs, 1893–1900).

52 **"horrified"** GI, Carter mss., VI.2.1.

52 **"The modus operandi in force"** Ibid.

52 **"I was young"** Ibid.

54 **"Bread, water and onions!"** Newberry to Edwards, November 28, 1892, Egyptian Exploration Society Archives XII d.54.

57 **"There was not the slightest idea"** GI, Carter mss., VI.2.1.

57 **"There were rumours abroad"** Ibid.

CHAPTER 5

59 **"From there we trailed"** GI, Carter mss., VI.2.1, quoted in Reeves and Taylor, *Howard Carter,* 32.

61 **"thoughtless implacable men"** Weigall, *Tutankhamen,* 175.

61 **"ground strewn with yellow fragments"** Ibid.

61 **"Fraser and Blackden returned"** GI, Carter mss., VI.2.1, quoted in Reeves and Taylor, *Howard Carter,* 32.

62 **Blackden and Fraser published "their" discovery** Blackden and Fraser, "Collection of Hieratic Graffiti from the Alabaster Quarries of Hat-Nub, Situated Near Tell El Amarna, Found December 28th, 1891, Copied September 1892," *Proceedings of the Society of Biblical Archaeology* XVI (January 1894): 73ff.

62 **"In all such archaeological research"** GI, Carter mss., VI.2.1.

62 **In 1923, Newberry and Fraser** For a follow-up of the quarrel still raging thirty years later, see T.G.H. James, "The Discovery and Identification of the Alabaster Quarries of Hatnub," *Cahier de recherches de l'Institut de Papyrologie et d'Égyptologie de Lille* 13 (Lille: Mélanges Jacques Jean Clère, 1991), 79–84.

63 **"In a week's time"** Ibid.

63 **"I resolutely avoided any possible entanglement"** Petrie to Hilda Urlin, between October 1896 and November 29, 1987, in possession of the Petrie family, quoted in Drower, *Flinders Petrie,* 233–237.

64 **"Overwork is a necessity"** Ibid.

64 **the remotest deserts in Syria** Ibid.

64 **"Petrie is a very bad sleeper"** Weigall to Newberry, undated [1902?], from a typescript sent to Hankey by Margaret Gardiner, quoted in Hankey, *A Passion,* 32.

65 **"I cannot again live"** Petrie to Hilda Urlin, between October 1896 and November 29, 1987, in possession of the Petrie family, quoted in Drower, *Flinders Petrie,* 233–237.

66 **Carter returned from leave** Breasted, *Pioneer,* 342. The colleagues involved are Percy Newberry and James Quibell.

PART THREE: THE WORLD OF
NEBKHEPERURE HEKAIUNUSHEMA TUTANKHAMUN

EPIGRAPH

67 **"Behold! A reed"** Inscribed walking stick, 71⅜ inches long. Find #229. For a photo of the find, see Nicholas Reeves, *The Complete Tutankhamun* (London: Thames & Hudson, 1995), 178.

CHAPTER 6

71 **"What may capture our interest"** Cyril Aldred, "Hairstyles and History," *MMA Bulletin* 15, no. 6 (February 1957): 141–147.

71 **It was a sign** Dominic Montserrat suggestively explores the Amarna period's meaning for modernity in *Akhenaten: History, Fantasy and Ancient Egypt* (London and New York: Routledge Press, 2000).

73 **"striking, almost beautiful"** Nicholas Reeves and Richard H. Wilkinson, *The Complete Valley of the Kings* (London: Thames & Hudson, 1996).

75 "visible and invisible reality" Jan Assman, *The Mind of Egypt: History and Meaning in the Time of the Pharaohs* (Cambridge, MA, and London: Harvard University Press, 2003), 216.

77 "marvelous but vulnerable" J. P. Allen, "Genesis in Egypt: The Philosophy of Ancient Egyptian Creation Accounts," *Yale Egyptological Studies* 2 (New Haven: Yale Egyptological Seminar, 1988): 313.

77 "Rib Hadda says to his lord" William Moran, *The Amarna Letters* (Baltimore and London: Johns Hopkins University Press, 1987), 185–190.

77 "Gulba is in danger" Ibid.

77 "If this year" Ibid.

77 "Rib Hadda says: whenever the king" Ibid.

79 "praised together with the perfect god" Cyril Aldred, *Akhenaten, Pharaoh of Egypt: A New Study* (London: Thames & Hudson, 1968), 94.

79 "Khuenaten is seated upon a throne" Carter to Newberry, April 7, 1892, GI, Newberry mss., I.8/3, quoted in James, *Howard Carter*, 43.

80 "I was one who was instructed" Aldred, *Akhenaten*, 94.

80 "The rows of complex columns" Norman de Garis Davies, *The Rock Tombs of El Amarna* (London: Egypt Exploration Fund, 1903–1908), 8.

CHAPTER 7

83 "I had to run" GI, Carter mss., VI.2.1, quoted in Reeves and Taylor, *Howard Carter*, 36.

83 "Excuse my shaky handwriting" Carter to Newberry, February 14, 1892, GI, Newberry correspondence 8/1.

84 "a subtle recognition of the facts" GI, Carter mss., VI.2.1, quoted in Reeves and Taylor, *Howard Carter*, 40.

85 "In the course of my work" Ibid.

89 Driving through traffic in a taxi On March 26, 1903, Carter brought Thutmosis IV's mummy to be examined by Grafton Elliot Smith in the presence of Lord Cromer.

89 "Under his acute perspicacity" GI, Carter mss., VI.2.1, quoted in Reeves and Taylor, *Howard Carter*, 40.

90 **"house on fire"** Hankey, *A Passion*, 26.

90 **"one worker held him down"** Drower, *Flinders Petrie*, 91.

90 **"A run of two to four miles"** Ibid.

91 **"Fragment. Neck and shoulders"** W. M. Flinders Petrie, *Tell el Amarna* (London: Methuen, 1894), 15–17. Also Aldred, *Akhenaten*, 54, and James, *Howard Carter*, 40–41. For photos of Carter's finds, see Aldred, *Akhenaten*, 36–37; and Reeves and Taylor, *Howard Carter*, 38–39. A selection of the fragments ("one lot") is held by the MMA Department of Egyptian Art.

94 **"with admirable freedom of the branching"** Petrie, *Tell el Amarna*, 14.

97 **"If staying out in the sun"** Moran, *The Amarna Letters*, 39.

97 **"I little thought how much"** Petrie, *Seventy Years in Archaeology*, quoted in Hankey, *A Passion*, 26.

PART FOUR: IN THE VALLEY OF THE KINGS

EPIGRAPH

99 **"I've been through the mill"** Frances Donaldson, *Edward VIII* (New York: Ballantine Books, 1974), 554.

CHAPTER 8

101 **white gloves and a tasseled fez** Hankey, *A Passion*, 47, for Weigall's sketch of Carter dressed as chief inspector of antiquities. For Egyptian government dress regulations, see p. 60 of this work.

102 **He could tell many stories** John Romer, *The Valley of the Kings* (New York: Henry Holt & Co., 1981), 195, for Carter's imaginative dinner companion; further details in the Andrews diary.

103 **"A few eroded steps"** GI, Carter mss., Notebook 16, Sketch VI, quoted in Reeves and Taylor, *Howard Carter*, 73.

104 **"Would that Egypt had no antiquities!"** Archibald H. Sayce, *Reminiscences* (London: Macmillan & Co., 1923), 285. For Cromer's political views and general outlook, see Evelyn Baring

(Earl of Cromer), *Modern Egypt,* Vols. I and II (London: Macmillan & Co., 1908).

106 **"I took my servant's blunderbuss"** James Bruce, *Travels to Discover the Source of the Nile* (Edinburgh, 1790); quoted in Romer, *The Valley,* 34.

107 **"the rain made it impracticable"** GI, Carter mss., VI.2.1.

109 **"in the innermost recesses"** Howard Carter, "A Tomb Prepared for Queen Hapshepsuit and Other Recent Discoveries at Thebes," *Journal of Egyptian Archaeology* 4 (1917), 107.

109 **"I have marked HC"** Ibid., 108.

109 **"I saw a shiny vertical line"** Howard Carter, *The Tomb of Tut.ankh.Amen,* Introduction by John Romer (London: Century Publishing Co., 1983), 9.

111 **"He is absolutely fearless"** Andrews diary, January 17, 1902.

113 **"I believe that henceforth"** Édouard Naville, *The Discovery of the Book of the Law Under King Josiah: An Egyptian Interpretation of the Biblical Account* (London: Society for Promoting Christian Knowledge, 1911), 46. [Microfilm. Master negative of Naville, Édouard, zp-699, Schiff Collection, xi, 46p, 19cm zp-699, no. 2, New York Public Library.]

113 **"I regret to tell you"** Edwards to Petrie, undated [1889?], Petrie Papers 9 (iv) 54, Petrie Museum, University College, London, quoted in Drower, *Flinders Petrie,* 281.

114 **"It is certainly quite remarkable"** Naville to the Egypt Exploration Fund Committee, February 27, 1898, Egyptian Exploration Society Archives XI a5.

114 **"I have been able to judge"** Naville to Edward Maunde Thompson, January 11, 1894, Egyptian Exploration Society Archives XVII.16.

114 **"Due possibly to Petrie's training"** GI, Carter mss., Notebook 16, "An Account of Myself," quoted in Winstone, *Howard Carter,* 54.

114 **"the temple setting"** GI, Carter mss., VI.2.1.

CHAPTER 9

116 **"The tomb proved to be 700"** GI, Carter mss., Notebook 16, Sketch VII, quoted in Reeves and Taylor, *Howard Carter,* 78.

117 **"Ramesseum. Northeast Wall of 2nd Temple"** Egypt Exploration Fund Archaeological Reports, *ASAE* 2 (1901–1903).

118 **"the pigeon on the right"** Carter to his mother, August 24, 1900, letter held by John Carter, quoted in Reeves and Taylor, *Howard Carter,* 58.

118 **An astonished colleague** Arthur Mace journal, February 1, 1900, Abydos, Egypt, quoted in Lee, *The Grand Piano.*

119 **Another colleague (Arthur Weigall)** Hankey, *A Passion,* 47.

119 **"the reis of the guards"** John Wilson to Charles Breasted, November 28, 1940, Chicago House Director's Office, Luxor, Egypt, quoted in James, *Howard Carter,* 151.

120 **Who is this Inspector** Quoted in James, *Howard Carter,* 89, from the newspaper *Le Phare d'Alexandrie.*

120 **Why would "a person of no importance"** Ibid., from the newspaper *L'Égypte.*

121 **"About three pm"** GI, Carter mss., V.148, Carter's complaint against visitors to Saqqara on January 8, 1905.

122 **"On finding one of them"** Ibid.

123 **"My Lord, I am exceedingly sorry"** GI, Carter mss., V.107.

123 **"Administration des Télégraphes"** See Reeves and Taylor, *Howard Carter,* 80, for a photo of this telegram.

124 **"to drive away these"** Quoted in James, *Howard Carter,* 119, from the newspaper *L'Égypte.*

124 **"Lord Cromer said"** GI, Carter mss., V.148, 33, verso.

125 **"In no disparaging sense"** Arthur Weigall, *A History of Events in Egypt from 1796 to 1914* (Edinburgh and London: W. Blackwood, 1915), 175, quoted in Hankey, *A Passion,* 216.

125 **"They had dry bread to eat"** Petrie, *Ten Years' Digging,* 128.

126 **"You are to come with me"** Maspero to Carter, February 3, 1905, GI, Carter mss., V.121.

126 **"I feel the humiliation"** Carter to Maspero, February 20, 1905, GI, Carter mss., V.130.

126 **"Pay no attention"** Davis to Carter, February 10, 1905, GI, Carter mss., V.124.

127 **"I cannot believe"** Carter to Davis, undated, GI, Carter mss., V.124.

127 **"I received your letter"** Davis to Carter, February 10, 1905, GI, Carter mss., V.124.

129 **Weigall privately circulated a caricature** See Hankey, *A Passion,* 126, for Weigall's sketch.

130 **"That is the really bad part"** Maspero to Carter, January 19, 1905, GI, Carter mss., V.148, 25f, quoted in James, Howard Carter, 122.

131 **The American Egyptologist James Breasted reported** Charles Breasted, *Pioneer,* 162.

132 **the Earl and Countess of Carnarvon** *Egyptian Gazette,* December 14, 1905, quoted in James, *Howard Carter,* 147.

PART FIVE: A USEFUL MAN

EPIGRAPH

133 **"I am off to the races!"** Carnarvon to Newberry, April 23, 1911, GI, Newberry correspondence, 7/90.

CHAPTER 10

136 **"mauvaise [*sic*] caractere"** GI, Carter mss., VI.2.1.

136 **"Living alone as I do"** Carter to Newberry, October 27, 1911, GI, Newberry mss., I.8/35.

136 **"I do so dislike"** Geanie Weigall diary, December 7, 1910–June 14, 1911, held by the Weigall family, quoted in Hankey, *A Passion,* 154.

137 **"I worked in the valley"** Lindsley Hall diary, February 7, 1923, MMA Department of Egyptian Art, quoted in Reeves and Taylor, *Howard Carter,* 154.

137 **"The man is unbearable"** James, *Howard Carter,* 240.

137 **"In the beginning"** Winstone, *Howard Carter,* 310. The remark was repeated to the author by Patricia Leatham, Lady Evelyn's daughter, in a March 1990 interview.

138 **"Friday Evening. I have been feeling"** Carnarvon to Carter, February 23, 1923, MMA Department of Egyptian Art.

139 **"Usually when I returned from school"** Henry Herbert Carnarvon, Sixth Earl of, *No Regrets: Memoirs of the Earl of Carnarvon* (London: Weidenfeld & Nicolson, 1976), 11.

141 **"frankly detested the classics"** Howard Carter and A. C. Mace,

The Discovery of the Tomb of Tutankhamen, with a Biographical Sketch of the Late Lord Carnarvon by Lady Burghclere (New York: Dover Publications, 1977), 10.

142 **"He was known to have pitted"** Gerald O'Farrell, *The Tutankhamun Deception* (New York: Pan Books, 2002), 52.

142 **"On one occasion"** Carter and Mace, *The Discovery of . . . with a Biographical Sketch,* 15.

144 **"We had the whole Devonshire party"** Andrews diary, January 18, 1908, quoted in Hankey, *A Passion,* 108.

145 **"It seems to me totally unnecessary"** Carnarvon, *No Regrets,* 115.

147 The one prediction Weigall, *Tutankhamen,* 88, quoted in Reeves, *Tutankhamun,* 157.

147 **"we stand between the eternity"** Amelia Edwards, *Pharaohs, Fellahs and Explorers* (New York: Harper & Brothers, 1900), 12.

148 As Weigall described it Hankey, *A Passion,* 109.

CHAPTER 11

149 **"At every step in Egypt"** Edwards, *Pharaohs,* 12–14.

151 a **"mystical potency"** GI, Carter's diary, November–December 1925.

151 **"Legrain is a fool"** Maspero to Weigall, December 28, 1908, Arthur Weigall Archive, held by Julie Hankey, quoted in Hankey, *A Passion,* 132.

152 **"Everyone—natives and foreigners"** Maspero to Legrain, March 23, 1911, Arthur Weigall Archive, held by Julie Hankey, quoted in Hankey, *A Passion,* 361, see fn 34.

152 **"Ayrton was not popular at night"** Smith to his mother, March 1908, Archives of American Art, Smithsonian Institution, Washington, D.C., correspondence of Joseph Lindon Smith.

153 **"By lamplight, therefore, the work"** Weigall, *Tutankhamen,* 146–150.

156 **"Imagination is a good servant"** Petrie, *Ten Years' Digging,* 156.

156 **"The warm, dry and motionless atmosphere"** GI, Carter mss., VI.2.1.

156 **"Many of the roof slabs"** Howard Carter, "Report of Work Done in Upper Egypt, 1902–1903, Edfu Temple," *ASAE* 4 (1903).

157 **"May 1901. Temple strutted"** Ibid.

157 **"159 L.E. prices for girders"** Ibid.

157 **He was not a great artist** Thomas Hoving, *Tutankhamun: The Untold Story* (New York: Simon & Schuster, 1978), 27.

158 **"On the left cheek"** Howard Carter, *The Tomb of Tut.ankh.Amen,* Vol. II (1927); Dr. Derry, Appendix I, "Report Upon the Examination of Tutankhamen's Mummy" (New York: Cooper Square Publishers, 1963). Also see F. F. Leek, *The Human Remains from the Tomb of Tut'ankhamun* (Oxford: Griffith Institute, 1972), 6.

159 **Before the discovery** I am indebted to Christine El Mahdy, who makes this point in *Tutankhamen: The Life and Death of the Boy-King* (New York: St. Martin's Griffin, 1999), 131. She states: "Efforts to wipe out his [Tutankhamun's] very existence had almost been successful, and had it not been for the discovery of the tomb, he would be an historical nonentity to this day."

159 **"I watched Helen Cunliffe-Owen"** Carnarvon, *No Regrets,* 129.

161 **He wrote in his autobiographical sketch** GI, Carter, "An Account of Myself," Notebook 15, Sketch II, 46, quoted in Winstone, *Howard Carter,* 53.

161 **"He doesn't hesitate to"** GI, Newberry correspondence, 33/31.

161 **"I have never accepted Carter"** Reisner to Howes (of the Boston Museum), October 9, 1924, Boston Museum of Fine Arts Department of Egyptian Art, quoted in Reeves and Taylor, *Howard Carter,* 161.

162 **If Carnarvon could be irritating** For a photo of a typical Carnarvon menu, see Reeves and Taylor, *Howard Carter,* 108.

PART SIX: A FINAL THROW OF THE DICE

EPIGRAPH

163 **"How did they meet?"** Denis Diderot, *Jacques the Fatalist* (London: Oxford World Classics, 1999), 1.

166 "Lord Carnarvon . . . discovered" Weigall, *Tutankhamen,* 140. For a photo of the find, see Reeves, *The Complete Tutankhamun,* 23.

168 "Towards the end of the work" Weigall to Griffith, October 1, 1908, GI, Griffith correspondence, 362, quoted in Hankey, *A Passion,* 127.

169 "It is grievous to think" Griffith to Weigall, October 2, 1908, Arthur Weigall Archive, quoted in Hankey, *A Passion,* 127.

169 "No single inscription" Alan H. Gardiner, "The Defeat of the Hyksos by Kamôse: The Carnarvon Tablet, no. 1," *Journal of Egyptian Archaeology* 3 (1916).

169 "at the time of the perfuming" Griffith's translation, found in George Edward Stanhope Molyneux Herbert, Fifth Earl of Carnarvon, and Howard Carter, *Five Years' Explorations at Thebes: A Record of Work Done 1907–1911* (London: Henry Frowde, 1912).

169 "I would rather discover" Carter, *The Discovery of . . . with a Biographical Sketch,* Vol. I, 29.

170 "After perhaps ten days work" Carnarvon and Carter, *Five Years';* see "Introduction by the Earl of Carnarvon."

171 "spoke to him as if" Arthur Mace to Winifred Mace, January 28, 1922, Mace Papers, held by Margaret Orr, quoted in James, *Howard Carter,* 283.

174 "fears the Valley" Theodore Davis et al., *Excavations: Biban el Moluk: The Tombs of Harmhabi and Touatânkhamanou* (London: Constable, 1912), 3. Carter refers to Davis's remark in *The Discovery of . . . with a Biographical Sketch,* Vol. I, 75.

174 the asker being Herbert Winlock For Winlock's analysis, see Herbert Winlock, "Materials Used at the Embalming of King Tūt-'ankh-Amūn," MMA Papers, New York, 1941.

175 Davis was preparing his volumes Davis, *Harmhabi and Touatânkhamanou.*

176 "The absence of officials" Carter, *The Discovery of . . . with a Biographical Sketch,* Vol. I, 79.

CHAPTER 13

181 "In the summer of 1922" Charles Breasted, *Pioneer,* 328–329.

182 "He granted that perhaps even Ibid.

182 "It is well known" James Breasted to his wife, November 27, 1925, University of Chicago, Oriental Institute, Director's Office correspondence, 1925.

183 "laid before him" Charles Breasted, *Pioneer,* 328–329.

183 "Some later, off-season time Ibid.

184 In her thought-provoking *Tutankhamen* El Mahdy, *Tutankhamen,* 205.

186 "In this area" Charles Breasted, *Pioneer,* 328–329.

186 "Now, said Carter" Ibid.

CHAPTER 14

188 "Hardly had I arrived" Carter, *The Tomb of Tut.ankh.Amen,* Introduction by John Romer, 49–55.

189 "Anything, literally anything" Ibid.

190 "At last have made" Ibid.

191 "Plunderers had entered it" Ibid.

191 "With trembling hands" Ibid.

EPILOGUE

193 "There were soldiers springing" Arthur Weigall for the *Daily Mail,* February [18?], 1923. The scene at the newly discovered tomb was similarly described in the *Daily Telegraph,* quoted in Hoving, *The Untold Story,* 153.

194 "strange rustling murmuring whispering sounds" James H. Breasted, "Some Experiences in the Tomb of Tetenkhamon" [microfilm: Z-6583 no. 13, Breasted, James Henry, 1865–1935] (Chicago: University of Chicago, 1923), Chicago University Alumni Pamphlets, no. 2.

198 The steward handed From the notes of Lee Keedick of Keedick's Lecture Bureau, who accompanied Carter during his Ameri-

can speaking tour. Mr. Keedick's son provided a copy to Hoving, *The Untold Story,* 330.

198 **"We found him repairing"** Caton-Thompson, *Mixed Memoirs,* 148.

198 **"a pair of jackals"** GI, Carter's diary, September 1928–April 1929; entry in question October 27, 1928.

SELECTED BIBLIOGRAPHY

Aldred, Cyril. *Akhenaten, Pharaoh of Egypt: A New Study.* London: Thames & Hudson, 1968.

———. "Hairstyles and History." *MMA Bulletin* (New Series) 15, no. 6 (February 1957).

Allen, J. P. "Genesis in Egypt: The Philosophy of Ancient Egyptian Creation Accounts," *Yale Egyptological Studies* 2 (New Haven: Yale Egyptological Seminar, 1988).

Andrews, Emma. Diary, "A Journal on the Bedawin, 1889–1912." American Philosophical Society, Philadelphia.

Baring, Evelyn (Earl of Cromer). *Modern Egypt.* 2 vols. London: Macmillan & Co., 1908.

Breasted, Charles. *Pioneer to the Past: The Story of James H. Breasted.* New York: Charles Scribner's Sons, 1943.

Breasted, James H. *Ancient Records of Egypt: Historical Documents,* Vols. I–IV. Chicago: University of Chicago Press, 1906.

Brier, Bob. *Egyptian Mummies: Unraveling the Secrets of an Ancient Art.* New York: Quill, William Morrow, 1994.

Carnarvon, Henry Herbert, Sixth Earl of. *No Regrets: Memoirs of the Earl of Carnarvon.* London: Weidenfeld & Nicolson, 1976.

Carter, Howard. "Report on the Tomb of Mentuhotep 1st, known as Bab El Hosan." *Annales du Service des Antiquités de l'Égypte* 2 (1901).

———. *The Tomb of Tut.ankh.Amen.* Introduction by John Romer. London: Century Publishing Co., 1983.

———. "A Tomb Prepared for Queen Hapshepsuit and Other Recent Discoveries at Thebes." *Journal of Egyptian Archaeology* 4 (London, 1917).

———, and A. C. Mace. *The Tomb of Tut.ankh.Amen,* Vol. I, 1923; Howard Carter, Vol. II, 1927; Howard Carter, Vol. III, 1933; 3 vols. New York: Cooper Square Publishers, 1963.

Caton-Thompson, Gertrude. *Mixed Memoirs.* Gateshead: Tyne & Wear, 1922.

Davies, Norman de Garis. *The Rock Tombs of El Amarna.* London: Egypt Exploration Fund, 1903–1908.

Davis, Theodore, et al. *Excavations, Biban el Moluk: The Tombs of Harmhabi and Touatânkhamanou.* London: Constable, 1912.

Drower, Margaret. *Flinders Petrie: A Life in Archaeology.* London: Victor Gollancz, 1985.

Edwards, Amelia. *Pharaohs, Fellahs and Explorers.* New York: Harper & Brothers, 1900.

El Mahdy, Christine. *Tutankhamen: The Life and Death of the Boy-King.* New York: St. Martin's Griffin, 1999.

Hankey, Julie. *A Passion for Egypt: Arthur Weigall, Tutankhamun and the Curse of the Pharaohs.* London and New York: I. B. Tauris Publishers, 2001.

Harrison, Robert T. *Imperialism in Egypt: Techniques of Domination.* Westport, CT, and London: Greenwood Press, 1995.

Hoving, Thomas. *Tutankhamun: The Untold Story.* New York: Simon & Schuster, 1978.

James, T.G.H. *Howard Carter: The Path to Tutankhamun.* Cairo: American University in Cairo Press, 1992.

Lee, Christopher C. *The Grand Piano Came by Camel: Arthur C. Mace, the Neglected Archaeologist.* Edinburgh: Mainstream Publishing, 1992.

Leek, F. F. *The Human Remains from the Tomb of Tut'ankhamun.* Oxford: Griffith Institute, 1972.

Montserrat, Dominic. *Akhenaten: History, Fantasy and Ancient Egypt.* London and New York: Routledge Press, 2000.

Moran, William. *The Amarna Letters.* Baltimore and London: Johns Hopkins University Press, 1987.

Naville, Édouard. *The Discovery of the Book of the Law Under King Josiah: An Egyptian Interpretation of the Biblical Account.* London: Society for Promoting Christian Knowledge, 1911.

Newberry, Percy. *Beni Hasan I–IV.* London: Egyptian Exploration Fund Archaeological Survey Memoirs, 1893–1900.

O' Connor, David, and Eric H. Cline, eds. *Amenhotep III: Perspectives on His Reign.* Ann Arbor: University of Michigan Press, 1998.

Peet, T. E. *The Great Tomb Robberies of the Twentieth Egyptian Dynasty.* Oxford: Clarendon Press 1930.

Petrie, W. M. Flinders. *Diospolis Parva: The Cemeteries of Abadiyeh and Hu, 1898–9.* London: Egyptian Exploration Fund, 1901.

———. *Seventy Years in Archaeology.* London: Methuen, 1931.

———. *Tell el Amarna.* London: Methuen, 1894.

———. *Ten Years' Digging in Egypt: The First Discovery of Tanis, Naukratis, Daphnae and Other Sites.* Chicago: University of Chicago Press, 1989; unchanged reprint, London: Methuen, 1891.

Redford, Donald. *The Akhenaten Temple Project.* Warminster, Eng.: Aris & Phillips, 1976.

Reeves, Nicholas. *The Complete Tutankhamun.* London: Thames & Hudson, 1995.

———, and John H. Taylor. *Howard Carter Before Tutankhamun.* London: British Museum Press, 1992.

———, and Richard H. Wilkinson, *The Complete Valley of the Kings.* London: Thames & Hudson, 1996.

Romer, John. *The Valley of the Kings.* New York: Henry Holt & Co., 1981.

Sayce, Archibald H. *Reminiscences.* London: Macmillan & Co., 1923.

Tyldesley, Joyce. *Judgement of the Pharaoh: Crime and Punishment in Ancient Egypt.* London: Weidenfeld & Nicolson, 2000.

Weigall, Arthur. *Tutankhamen and Other Essays.* Port Washington, NY and London: Kennikat Press, 1924; reissued 1970.

Winlock, Herbert E. "Materials Used at the Embalming of King Tūt-'ankh-Amūn." New York: MMA Papers, 1941.

Winstone, H.V.F. *Howard Carter and the Discovery of the Tomb of Tutankhamun.* London: Constable, 1991.

INDEX

ABOUT THE TYPE

This book was set in Bulmer, a typeface designed
in the late eighteenth century by the London
type-cutter William Martin. The typeface was
created especially for the Shakespeare Press, directed
by William Bulmer; hence, the font's name. Bulmer
is considered to be a transitional typeface, containing
characteristics of old-style and modern designs. It
is recognized for its elegantly proportioned letters,
with their long ascenders and descenders.